BEST SELLER OF
Stand As A King and Rule As A Queen

*30 Minutes Thursdays *90/10 Rule *Planting The Seeds.

3 TIPS TO CONFLICT RESOLUTION

Harrison S. Mungal, Ph.D., Psy.D

Team2

3 Tips To Conflict Resolution In Relationships

Copyright © 2025 Harrison S. Mungal

All rights reserved. Neither this publication nor any part of this publication may be reproduced or transmitted in any form or by any means, electronic or mechanical, including photocopying, recording or any information storage and retrieval system, without permission in writing from the author.

Contact author via email:
hsmungal@hotmail.com
info@agetoage.ca
www.agetoage.ca
www.harrisonmungal.com
www.harrisonmungalbooks.com
Facebook: Harrison Mungal
Twitter: AgeToAgeInc1
LinkedIn: Harrison Mungal, Ph.D., PsyD
YouTube: Harrison Mungal
Phone: 905-533-1334

the AUTHOR

Harrison Sharma Mungal, *BTh, MCC, MSW, PhD, PsyD*

Harrison Sharma Mungal, possessing dual doctoral distinctions in Clinical Psychology and Philosophy in Social Work, demonstrates an unwavering commitment to ameliorating the well-being of his clients. Renowned internationally for his profound insights into cognitive therapy, his expertise spans mental health, addiction, relationships, and family dynamics.

In his role as a highly sought-after workshop presenter, Dr. Mungal extends his practical approach to assisting individuals, couples, families, and corporations. His global influence is evident through engaging presentations at conferences, seminars, and media platforms, where he adeptly integrates humor and enthusiasm into nuanced discussions on mental health, addiction, relationships, and parenting.

Dr. Mungal's innovative and scientifically grounded methodology has garnered acclaim, earning him accolades from diverse institutions. He extends his influence through offering training and consultations to a wide array of community partners, including esteemed professionals in the medical, social work, first responder, law enforcement, and senior management domains.

Actively involved in pioneering cognitive research, Dr. Mungal leads ground-breaking studies addressing mental health challenges such as addiction, psychosis, anxiety, and depression. His work includes the exploration of practical applications, exemplified by initiatives like music therapy for schizophrenia, substance abuse and addictions in the food service industry, and vaccination protocols for young children.

With over two decades of professional acumen, Dr. Mungal has left an indelible mark on the fields of mental health and psychiatry, providing services to diverse communities impacted by brain injuries, refugees, victims of warfare, and individuals in crisis. His pragmatic therapeutic repertoire encompasses evidence-based treatments like Cognitive Behavioural Therapy (CBT), Cognitive Processing Therapy (CPT), Dialectical Behavioural Therapy (DBT), Thought Developmental Practice (TDP) and Acceptance and Commitment Therapy (ACT).

HARRISON
and
KATHLEEN

Harrison and Kathleen Mungal have built their lives on a foundation of faith, love, and a deep commitment to family. With over 35 years of a strong and successful marriage, they have nurtured a beautiful family that includes seven children, in-laws, and multiple grandchildren. Their devotion to the Lord is at the heart of their journey, and they actively serve in their local churches, carrying forward their passion for ministry.

Together, Harrison and Kathleen have played pivotal roles in church planting, pastoral leadership, and missionary work. As missionaries during the War in Croatia from 1994 to 1997, they ministered in challenging circumstances, spreading the gospel with unwavering faith. Over the years, they pastored in four churches, planted two congregations, and established a Bible college, which they led for over a decade. Their transition into mental health and addictions counseling was a natural extension of their heart for healing, combining their pastoral experience with practical tools to support individuals and families.

Their ministry spans the globe, speaking in churches worldwide on topics related to relationships, marriage, parenting, mental health, addictions, and the intersection of spirituality and psychology. Harrison is widely respected for his ability to blend biblical truths with scientific insights, bringing a unique "psychology twist" to his therapeutic approach. He explains that God created us as Body, Soul (mind, will, and emotions), and Spirit, and while physical and spiritual support are crucial, "the soul is where people are wounded and is in need of healing."

Harrison's expertise has been sought after by numerous media outlets, including appearances on *700 Club Canada* and *100 Huntley Street*. His wisdom has been shared in prestigious institutions, such as the Attorney General of Canada, police departments, hospitals, community agencies, and churches. His contributions have earned him widespread recognition from local authorities, police departments, mayors, community leaders, and countless families.

Through their life's work, Harrison and Kathleen have demonstrated an unwavering commitment to service—integrating faith, wisdom, and compassion to positively impact individuals, couples, and families. Their journey stands as a testament to the power of love, faith, and the pursuit of healing for those in need.

Table of Contents

Introduction 13
Conflict Resolutions 19
   Learning To Stand Together 19
      1. Pause Before Reacting 28
      2. Use A Secret Word To Defuse Tension 28
      3. Apply The 90/10 Rule 29
      4. Plant The Seed Instead Of Demanding An Explanation 29
      5. Shock The Brain: Interrupt Conflict With Love 29
      6. Set Boundaries Around Heated Topics 30
      7. Give Each Other Space When Necessary 30
      8. Leave Conversations On A Positive Note 30
      9. Focus On Solutions, Not Winning 30
      10. Make Sure Love Always Wins 31
   Understanding Conflict 33
      Why It Happens? 33
      1. Recognize That Conflict Is Normal 42
      2. Identify The Root Cause 42
      3. Pause Before Reacting 43

- 4. Avoid Making Conflict Personal 43
- 5. Be Open To Compromise 44
- 6. Understand That Conflict Often Has A History 44
- 7. Use Conflict To Strengthen Connection 45

30 Minutes Thursdays 47
  How Does It Work? 51
    Step 1: Bringing Up The Issue Without Emotion .. 51
    Step 2: Finding A Solution Together 52
    Step 3: Handling Unresolved Topics 52
    Tips To Remember: 54

90/10 Rule 57
  1. Start Conversations With Gratitude 76
  2. Make Appreciation A Daily Habit 76
  3. Frame Criticism Gently 76
  4. Leave Conversations On A Positive Note 76
  5. Avoid Keeping Score 77
  6. Create Rituals For Connection 77
  7. Know When To Pause 77
  8. Reframe Conflict As A Team Effort 77
  9. Understand Each Other's Love Languages 77
  10. Condition The Mind To Focus On Strengths .. 78

Planting The Seed 79
  Tips To Remember: 91

1. Pause Before Reacting 91

2. Choose The Right Moment 92

3. Frame It As A Passing Thought 92

4. Redirect The Conversation 92

5. Trust The Reflection Process 93

6. Recognize Patterns & Set Boundaries 93

7. Avoid Over-Explaining Or Seeking Justification 93

8. Show Consistent Positivity 94

Shock The Brain 97

Choosing Battles Wisely 107

Is The Argument Worth It? 107

1. Ask Yourself: Is This Worth The Emotional Toll? 117

2. Recognize When Exhaustion Or Stress Is Driving Conflict 118

3. Don't Turn Every Personality Difference Into A Problem 118

4. Let Go Of The Need To Be Right 119

5. Focus On Solutions, Not Frustration 119

6. Use Humor To Diffuse Small Conflicts 120

7. Protect Emotional Intimacy Over Proving A Point 120

Effective Communication 123

Speaking With Love And Clarity 123

Tips To Remember: 132

Separating The Problem 137

   Problems Are Not Enemies 137

   1. Identify The Root Cause 140

   2. Pause Before Responding 140

   3. Talk Like A Team, Not Opponents 141

   4. Make Problem-Solving A Priority 141

   5. Remove Emotional "Leeches" From Your Relationship 142

   6. Strengthen Your Partnership Through Respect 142

Common Ground 145

   Compromise 145

   1. Prioritize Unity Over Winning 151

   2. Recognize Your Differences Without Trying To Change Each Other 151

   3. Identify Non-Negotiables And Flexible Areas . 151

   4. Keep Communication Open And Respectful .. 152

   5. Seek God's Guidance In Difficult Decisions ... 152

   6. Reaffirm Your Commitment After Every Compromise 153

Love Over Conflict 155

   Avoid Damaging Emotional Security 155

   1. Pause Before Engaging In Conflict 161

   2. Focus On The Bigger Picture 162

3. Create Safe Spaces For Communication 162

4. Let Small Frustrations Go To Protect Unity 163

5. Replace Negative Moments With Positive Intentionality 163

6. Pray Together For Strength And Guidance...... 163

Putting Closure To The Past 165

You Past Does Not Define Your 165

1. Acknowledge What Happened Without Letting It Define The Future 172

2. Identify If Any Lingering Resentment Remains 173

3. Focus On Solutions Instead Of Just Emotions 173

4. Give Each Other The Benefit Of The Doubt . 173

5. Practice Symbolic Closure 174

6. Replace Negative Memories With New Positive Experiences 174

7. Commit To Growth, Not Perfection................. 174

Conclusion 177

References 181

INTRODUCTION

Conflict is a natural part of any relationship, but how we handle it determines whether love grows stronger or begins to erode. Disagreements are bound to happen—two individuals with unique perspectives, experiences, and emotions will not always see things the same way. But conflict does not have to mean division. It can be an opportunity for deeper understanding, growth, and connection.

This book will help you understand that every relationship experience conflict, but it's how you handle conflict that creates a healthy, lasting connection. Through the challenges of raising seven children and navigating the complexities of our different cultural and ethnic backgrounds, Kathleen and I have learned that conflict can either divide or strengthen a relationship depending on how it is managed. We have discovered

Introduction

three key strategies that have helped us stand together, grow through challenges, and cultivate a bond built on trust, understanding, and love.

Standing together in the face of disagreement is one of the most valuable lessons a couple can learn. Instead of seeing conflict as something that drives distance, couples can learn to stand together—choosing unity over division, mutual respect over frustration, and teamwork over isolation. Conflict resolution is not about proving a point or winning an argument; it's about ensuring that love stays the foundation even in the toughest moments.

Understanding why conflict happens is the first step to resolving it. Most disagreements don't arise from a single moment, but from unspoken frustrations, unmet expectations, or lingering emotional wounds. When couples recognize the patterns behind conflict, they can address the real issues rather than reacting to symptoms. This means asking, why does this argument keep happening? instead of why are we fighting again? Reflection leads to clarity, and clarity leads to healthier conversations.

Not all arguments need to be fought. Some moments of frustration will pass on their own, while others require deeper discussion. Choosing battles wisely helps couples protect their emotional energy, ensuring that only meaningful conversations take center stage. By asking, is this worth the tension? couples can prevent unnecessary disputes from overshadowing love.

How we speak during conflict is just as important as what we say. Effective communication—speaking with love and clarity—turns arguments into conversations. Hurtful words can leave lasting wounds, but careful, thoughtful dialogue can create understanding. Choosing warmth and intentional phrasing ensures that discussions lead to solutions rather than defensiveness.

One of the biggest mistakes couples make is treating the problem as the person—allowing the issue to feel like an attack rather than an obstacle that can be faced together.

Separating the problem from the relationship is crucial. When couples work as a team against the challenge instead of against each other, conflict resolution becomes a moment of shared strength rather than emotional distance.

Conflict does not need to end in resentment—it can end in common ground and compromise. A healthy relationship is not built on forcing one person to agree with the other, but on finding solutions that honor both perspectives. Compromise is not a loss; it's a decision to prioritize connection over stubbornness.

For many couples, past conflicts resurface, creating emotional baggage that weighs down future discussions.

Putting closure to the past is essential for emotional freedom—reminding each other that past mistakes do not define the present. Healing means letting go, choosing forgiveness, and ensuring that love moves forward rather than staying stuck in old wounds.

Love should always be stronger than conflict. The greatest danger in unresolved conflict is damaging emotional security, making partners feel unheard, unsafe, or disconnected. Relationships thrive when couples protect emotional safety, ensuring that disagreements never make love feel unstable. Conflict should lead to understanding, not fear.

Several strategies can help couples manage conflict with intention rather than reaction. Setting aside 30 minutes on Thursdays for discussions ensures that concerns are addressed at the right time, not in the heat of frustration. Allowing conversations to unfold as discussions rather than explanations prevents defensiveness, keeping communication open instead of argumentative.

The 90/10 rule reminds couples that love should always outweigh concern. If 90 percent of a conversation is built on appreciation and only 10 percent is devoted to addressing concerns, love remains the central focus. This conditions the mind to be positive, ensuring that frustration never defines the relationship.

Another powerful tool in conflict resolution is planting the seed—introducing concerns lightly and allowing them to settle in the mind rather than demanding immediate explanations. This allows reflection to occur naturally, preventing unnecessary tension.

Sometimes, patterns of conflict need to be disrupted entirely. Shocking the brain—changing your thinking—can shift an argument into a moment of reconnection. Instead of matching frustration with frustration, couples can interrupt the cycle by doing something unexpected—hugging, laughing, or redirecting the conversation with warmth. This teaches the brain that love should always lead, even when emotions are high.

This book will explore how couples can stand together, using several examples from Kathleen and me to illustrate how we navigate conflict with wisdom and ensure that disagreements lead to growth rather than harm. Through real-life experiences, we've learned that challenges don't have to create division—they can strengthen connection when handled with care and understanding. Because love should always guide the way, ruling over conflict—not the other way around.

CONFLICT RESOLUTIONS

Learning To Stand Together

Conflict is an inevitable part of marriage. No two individuals, no matter how deeply they love each other, will always see things the same way or react to situations identically. But conflict itself is not the problem—it's how couples handle disagreements that determines the strength of their relationship. Resolving conflicts is not about proving who is right or wrong, but about protecting our love, ensuring mutual respect, and standing together rather than allowing difficulties to divide us.

Marriage is a beautiful journey, but it comes with real struggles that young and old couples alike must navigate. Through trial, error, and growth, we've developed ways on how to tackle them without allowing them to weaken our relationship.

Many couples—both young and old—struggle with differences in conflict resolution styles. I am more emotionally expressive, while Kathleen needs time to process her thoughts before discussing them. Early on in our marriage, this caused tension. I wanted to resolve things right away, while she felt overwhelmed by immediate conversations. Over time, we learned to adjust to each other's emotional needs, ensuring that I felt heard, while Kathleen had space to process things without shutting her out.

We have learned that marriage is not about avoiding challenges—it's about facing them together. Whether newly married or decades into the journey, couples must communicate, compromise, and prioritize love above all else. Struggles do not have to break a relationship—they can be opportunities to build deeper understanding, strengthen the bond, and grow together in ways that make love last a lifetime.

While love is the foundation, it doesn't automatically eliminate the challenges that arise from differences. We all face our fair share of conflicts—some small, others significant—but through trial and error, we learn that understanding, patience, and communication are the keys to navigating the ups and downs of life together.

We've realized that love alone isn't enough to navigate the inevitable challenges we face. Differences in beliefs, habits, food preferences, behaviours, and even daily routines are areas where we adjust, compromise, and work together to keep our relationships strong.

One of the first challenges we've faced was how we handled conflict itself. I grew up in an environment were talking things out was crucial, but Kathleen preferred to process situations internally before discussing them. Early on, this difference led to moments of frustration. If we had a disagreement, I wanted to resolve it immediately, whereas Kathleen needed time to think through her feelings before engaging in the conversation. This often resulted in me feeling like she was avoiding the issue, while she felt pressured by my need to talk things through quickly. Over time, we learned that instead of forcing each other into our own way of handling conflict, we had to find a balance—allowing space for reflection without letting issues linger unresolved.

As marriages grow, so would the differences in emotional expressions. One person may tend to process emotions internally before discussing them, while the other may prefer to talk things through right away. This can cause misunderstandings—a quiet approach can be misunderstood as emotional distance, which can be overwhelmed by immediate discussions. We must work on adjusting to each other's emotional needs, ensuring that you spouse feels heard, and had sufficient space to process their thoughts without shutting them out.

One common issue is adjusting to living together. When Kathleen and I first got married, we had to learn how to blend our habits, routines, and personal preferences into a shared space. Suddenly, small things—like how to organize the kitchen, how much clutter was acceptable, and even how to spend free time—became topics of discussion (and sometimes frustration). I remember one time I wanted everything in the house perfectly neat, while Kathleen felt comfortable with a bit of controlled chaos. We had to learn the balance between respecting each other's space while ensuring our home felt like a place of peace for both of us.

Another issue couples encounter is adjusting to different levels of independence. Before marriage, we were used to making decisions for ourselves. After marriage, our choices impacted each other—whether financially, emotionally, or even socially. One person may be great at planning ahead, while the other may tend to be more spontaneous. This can lead to frustration, especially when you make last-minute plans and forgot to discuss it with you spouse. They may feel like they are not considered and was restricted. Over time, we learned the importance of checking in with each other before making decisions, not as a form of control, but as a way to honour our partnership.

Keeping romance alive through the years becomes a real challenge. As responsibilities increase—raising seven children, managing my career, handling family obligations—it's easy for the emotional connection to take a backseat. We've faced this struggle when we had our seventh child. Our schedules were packed, and instead of investing time in each other, we were constantly focused on everything around us.

We were pastoring, running a Bible college, travelling to different churches, guest speaker at seminars, conferences, crusades and studying. Date nights became rare, meaningful conversations were rushed, and eventually, we felt the emotional distance creeping in. We had to be intentional about prioritizing our relationship, ensuring that even in the busyness of life, we kept our love strong.

A difficult challenge I faces was letting go of control as our children grew up and start their own families. We've had to learn this lesson firsthand when our kids became adults and started relationships of their own. It's natural to want to guide and protect them, but we had to let them make their own choices, trusting that they would build their own strong marriages just as we had done. At times, it was hard not to step in or offer advice, but we recognized that our role had changed—we were now supporters rather than decision-makers in their lives. This created conflict at times when I felt Kathleen was parenting me to let go.

Another challenge most couples face is the differences in financial management. One may be a meticulous planner, always thinking ahead, while the other tend to focus on financial flexibility. Early in our marriage, this led to heated discussions when I made purchases without consulting Kathleen, not realizing the stress it caused her. In fact, I hid $10,000.00 from her. We had to find a system that worked for both of us—ensuring that finances were handled wisely while still allowing room for some spontaneity.

Finances were hot-button issue in our relationship for many years and sometimes pops up from time to time. I am cautious, disciplined, and like to plan ahead when it comes to money, while Kathleen is more spontaneous in her spending habits. Early on, this created stress—I wanted to stick to a budget, while she felt restricted by financial constraints. Our biggest argument happened when we did not make financial decisions together, respecting each other's perspectives rather than letting money drive a wedge between us.

Health concerns and aging become another challenge. As the years pass, energy levels shift, health may decline, and responsibilities within the marriage need adjustment. We realize that we had to be patient with each other, support each other through physical changes, and ensure that we remained a team even in difficult seasons.

One of the sources of conflict for couples is misaligned expectations. Before getting married, we all have our own ideas of what life together would look like—how responsibilities would be divided, how affection would be expressed, and how decisions would be made. Most couples think they understand each other's expectations, only to find out that reality looked very different.

I thought certain household tasks would just "naturally" fall into place, but Kathleen had a structured approach that required mutual effort. She expected me to help with chores without needing reminders, while I assumed she would tell me when she needed help. These misunderstandings led to frustration, with both of us feeling unheard. We realized that unspoken expectations lead to disappointment, and instead of assuming, we needed to clearly communicate our needs and responsibilities.

Differences in personalities and habits are another source of conflict. Some individuals are more naturally organized, detail-oriented, and structured, while others have a more relaxed, flexible approach. This can lead to tension in how you handled everyday tasks—from scheduling outings to managing your home. At one point, Kathleen felt overwhelmed by the planning that fell entirely on her, while I, unaware, thought she enjoyed taking the lead. We had to sit down and reassess how to share the mental load, ensuring that neither of us felt like we were carrying the burden alone.

The challenge of balancing family relationships can also bring moments of tension. Families—whether in-laws, extended relatives, or even your own parents—come with their own expectations, traditions, and ways of doing things. We had to learn how to set boundaries with our families while maintaining respect and love. There were times when external opinions influenced our decisions, causing unnecessary stress between us. We had to remind ourselves that while family is important, our marriage came first, and it was up to us to decide how we wanted to navigate our life together.

Another adjustment is the differences in cultural and family traditions. I recall one particular moment when Kathleen and I were planning our first big family gathering. In my mind, I had a clear idea of how things should be done—food should be served a certain way, schedules should be loose and flexible, and conversations should flow naturally. Kathleen, however, had a structured approach—she wanted things planned ahead of time, schedules laid out, and clear expectations for the event.

I grew up expecting all types of meats, curries, rotis and spicy food, while Kathleen was raised with roast turkey or beef, mashed potatoes, and salads. I grew up where cows were holy so never ate beef. We clashed over the preparations, and what should have been an exciting time turned into frustration over small differences in how we saw things. Eventually, we realized that instead of fighting over which way was *better*, the real solution was in blending our ideas to create an event that suited both of our personalities.

The challenges of learning to let go of past conflicts can be difficult. Couples often struggle with bringing up old disagreements during new arguments, making resolution difficult. There were times when we've let past frustrations influence our present conversations, using words that reopened old wounds. We had to actively practice forgiveness, understanding that dragging past conflicts into new discussions only deepened resentment. Instead, we chose to move forward rather than dwell on past mistakes.

Through all these experiences, we've realized that conflict is not the enemy—miscommunication and unresolved frustrations are. By recognizing each other's perspectives, making compromises, and choosing unity over division, we've built a marriage that stands strong even through disagreements. Love does not mean avoiding conflict—it means handling it with care, respect, and a willingness to grow together.

One of the biggest lessons we learned is that conflict does not mean failure—it means an opportunity for understanding. The times when we disagreed were never about proving who was *right*—they were about working toward solutions that allowed both of us to feel valued and respected. Holding onto unresolved issues only made tension worse, while learning to release frustrations and approach conversations with patience helped us heal from misunderstandings and build trust.

Conflict is a natural part of any relationship, but how couples handle disagreements determines whether they grow stronger or drift apart.

TIPS TO REMEMBER:

1. Pause Before Reacting

- Bite your tongue—not every disagreement needs an immediate response.
- Take a breath before saying something in the heat of the moment.
- If emotions are running high, step away and revisit the conversation later with a clearer mindset.

2. Use a Secret Word to Defuse Tension

- If conflict arises in public or around others, have a lighthearted, private word that signals to pause the disagreement.
- This prevents frustration from escalating and keeps respect intact even in social settings.

3. Apply the 90/10 Rule

- 90% positive affirmations, 10% concerns—ensure appreciation outweighs criticism.
- Instead of saying, *"You never help around the house,"* try, *"I really appreciate everything you do. I'd love if we could find a better balance with chores."*

4. Plant the Seed Instead of Demanding an Explanation

- Instead of arguing when hurtful words are spoken, wait a few days before casually bringing it up.
- Say, *"The other day, when you said ___, that bothered me. But, needless to say, that was a few days ago."*
- Change the topic immediately—this lets your partner reflect without getting defensive.

5. Shock the Brain: Interrupt Conflict with Love

- Instead of matching frustration with frustration, do something unexpected:
    - Hug your partner during an argument.
    - Crack a joke to lighten the mood.
    - Kiss them to remind yourselves that love is stronger than the disagreement.

6. Set Boundaries Around Heated Topics

- Not every conversation needs to happen right now—some discussions are best saved for private, calm moments.
- Agree to postpone difficult conversations until emotions settle.

7. Give Each Other Space When Necessary

- If frustration is mounting, walk away rather than engage in negativity.
- Agree on signals that indicate "Let's revisit this later" instead of forcing a discussion in the wrong moment.

8. Leave Conversations on a Positive Note

- Even after difficult discussions, always end with reassurance:
    - *"I love you, and we'll figure this out."*
    - *"I'm grateful for us, even when we don't see things the same way."*
- This reinforces emotional security, preventing lingering resentment.

9. Focus on Solutions, Not Winning

- Conflict isn't a battle to win—it's an opportunity to strengthen understanding.

- Instead of proving a point, ask: *"How can we solve this together?"*

10. Make Sure Love Always Wins

- Don't let conflict take control of your relationship—choose each other over the argument.
- Recognize that disagreements come and go, but your commitment remains.

UNDERSTANDING CONFLICT

Why It Happens?

Conflict often arises from differences in personality, unmet expectations, financial strain, parenting choices, stress, and communication styles. Some conflicts come and go, while others persist if not addressed properly. There are moments when disagreement seemed like an emotional battlefield, but through growth, experience, and intentional effort, we learned that conflict, when handled wisely, can deepen trust and strengthen emotional connection. Understanding conflict is essential for maintaining a healthy and fulfilling relationship.

Understanding Conflict

Conflict arises in every marriage, not because love is absent, but because differences in thoughts, emotions, and expectations naturally create moments of tension. We all have experienced firsthand that conflict is not the enemy—miscommunication and unresolved frustrations are. Learning how to identify conflict and manage it effectively allows couples to grow rather than become divided by their disagreements.

Understanding conflict means recognizing that it is inevitable, but manageable. Kathleen and I have learned that love does not eliminate differences—it simply makes resolution possible. By embracing effective communication, recognizing emotional triggers, expressing expectations clearly, and approaching conflict with problem-solving rather than blame, couples can create stronger, more resilient relationships built on mutual trust, respect, and emotional security.

Conflict in marriage is inevitable and understanding why it happens is one of the most critical steps toward resolving it effectively. We all have encountered many moments of tension, and through experience, and learned that conflict itself is not the real problem—how we respond to it determines whether it weakens or strengthens our relationship.

One common causes of conflict are differences in communication styles. Research suggests that individuals communicate based on learned behaviours, emotional influences, and personal experiences (Markman et al., 2020). Our approach to discussing issues can be completely different than our spouse. Some may prefer to process their emotions before engaging in a discussion, while others may want to address problems immediately. This can lead to frustration—feeling rushed into conversations or dismissed when issues weren't resolved quickly.

Over time, we've learned that conflict resolution required adjusting to each other's communication preferences rather than expecting one person to conform entirely. By acknowledging our differences, we create a more balanced approach to discussing disagreements, ensuring that both feels heard and valued.

Emotional triggers play a significant role in how conflict escalates. When people are under stress, their emotional responses tend to intensify, often making minor issues seem much larger than they really are (Johnson & Green, 2021). You may notice that during particularly overwhelming seasons—whether financial strain, parenting challenges, or career demands—your ability to handle conflict calmly decreases.

Simple misunderstandings feel personal, and frustration surfaced more quickly. Recognizing this pattern allows you to pause and assess whether your emotions are heightened by external stressors rather than the actual issue at hand. Research suggests that self-awareness in emotionally charged situations improves problem-solving and reduces impulsive reactions (Smith et al., 2022). By practicing mindful communication, you'll become more intentional about addressing problems with clarity rather than emotional intensity.

Another source of conflict comes from unspoken expectations. Many couples assume their partner should instinctively understand their needs and desires yet failing to communicate these expectations often leads to disappointment. In the early stage of marriage, particularly when it comes to household responsibilities, it's easy to assume that certain tasks would fall naturally into place without needing detailed discussions, but that is not always the case, as some spouses may expect a more structured division of labour.

When responsibilities feel uneven, frustration will arise—not because you don't care, but because you haven't communicated your expectations clearly. Research highlights that couples who openly express their needs without assumption foster deeper trust and reduce misunderstandings (Smith et al., 2022). When we learn to voice our expectations rather than assume them, conflicts over responsibilities becomes much easier to navigate.

Cultural and family influences plays a critical role in relationship conflicts. Couples bring deeply ingrained beliefs and traditions into their marriage, often shaped by childhood environments and family dynamics (Markman et al., 2020).

We've faced challenges in blending our family influences, particularly regarding holiday traditions, personal values, and ways of handling difficult situations. At times, what seemed normal to one of us felt unfamiliar or even uncomfortable to the other. Instead of allowing these differences to become a barrier, we approached them as opportunities to learn from each other and create a shared foundation that respected both our backgrounds. Acknowledging cultural influences helped us embrace compromise rather than conflict, fostering mutual appreciation for what shaped us individually while prioritizing unity as a couple.

Many couples experience conflict because of differences in family dynamics and traditions. Kathleen and I quickly noticed that our family expectations shaped how we approached marriage. The way we expressed love, communicated during difficult times, and even handled financial decisions were deeply influenced by how we grew up. In the early years, we found that certain habits—like how to celebrate holidays or manage responsibilities—were sources of misunderstanding simply because they were approached differently in our families.

Problem-solving is the key to successful conflict resolution. Rather than focusing solely on the argument itself, couples must work toward solutions that honour both perspectives. Studies show that approaching disagreements with the mindset of teamwork rather than opposition fosters stronger emotional connections (Johnson & Green, 2021). You must implement intentional strategies in your discussions—asking solution-driven questions like, *"How can we prevent this issue from happening again?"* rather than dwelling on *"Why did this happen?"* This approach shifted our focus toward practical resolutions instead of repeating cycles of frustration.

One moment of conflict arose during our first year of marriage when I wanted to plan our holiday gathering weeks in advance, while Kathleen was used to a more spontaneous approach—deciding plans closer to the actual date. The issue wasn't that either of us was *wrong*; it was that we were coming from two separate experiences. At first, frustration built up because neither of us saw why the other person handled it differently. Once we recognized that this conflict wasn't personal—it was about different expectations—we worked on blending our traditions instead of trying to "correct" each other's approach.

Conflict often happens not because couples dislike each other, but because external pressures amplify emotional reactions. You will face moments when stress from work, financial concerns, or parenting struggles make small disagreements seem much bigger than they actually were. There will be nights when exhaustion will make simple conversations feel overwhelming, leading to tension over things that normally wouldn't have bothered you.

For example, disagreement over dividing daily responsibilities. Some people may feel overwhelmed managing work, family obligations, and household tasks, while others haven't fully recognized how much the other is carrying on their shoulders. You may feel frustrated handling more than expected, while your spouse assumed you have a balanced routine. The issue may not relate to either person personally—but the stress influencing how the situation perceived. Once you take time to step back and identify the actual source—external exhaustion rather than a lack of effort—you will be able to approach the conversation with more patience, working together to redistribute tasks in a way that felt fair.

One of the leading causes of conflict is assuming instead of clarifying. We've experienced this firsthand when it came to how we interpreted each other's emotions. I express my feelings immediately and openly, while Kathleen tends to process her emotions before verbalizing them. In the beginning, this difference led to misunderstandings—I thought she was emotionally distant when she wasn't ready to talk, while she assumed I was overreacting when I expressed frustration right away.

Understanding Conflict

The turning point came when we stopped assuming and started asking questions before drawing conclusions. Instead of me thinking, *"She doesn't care,"* I would ask, *"Do you need time before discussing this?"* Likewise, instead of she thinking, *"He's overreacting,"* She would ask, *"Do you need me to listen right now or help problem-solve?"* These simple changes helped us navigate emotional discussions without turning misunderstandings into deeper arguments.

Many conflicts happen because couples expect certain things from each other but never express them directly. One spouse may assume that the other would take the lead on certain tasks, while the other assume the same. There is an expectation that one would remind the other if help is needed. However, when expectations is not explicitly discussed, frustration builds up on both sides.

Instead of letting resentment grow, we made a habit of verbalizing expectations rather than assuming the other person automatically knew what needed to be done. We have to create a system where we check in with each other about what needs support rather than assuming responsibilities would naturally fall into place. This simple adjustment helps eliminate unnecessary tension, ensuring that both people feel heard and valued.

One challenge many couples face—is the tendency to carry unresolved conflict into new discussions. There were times when past frustrations resurfaced even when we were discussing something entirely different. If a disagreement wasn't fully resolved, it would show up again in future conversations, making small frustrations feel much larger than they actually were.

One major realization we had was that conflict should be fully resolved rather than carried over into new moments. We made a commitment to close the door on past arguments rather than reopening them. Instead of bringing up previous disagreements when discussing new issues, we kept our focus on the present, ensuring that past mistakes didn't dictate the tone of new conversations.

Conflict happens for a reason, and rather than fearing disagreements, we embraced them as opportunities to grow together. By recognizing that differences in perspective, stress, assumptions, expectations, and past experiences influence how we engage with each other, we were able to approach discussions with greater patience, problem-solving skills, and teamwork.

Understanding conflict means knowing that it isn't about proving who is right—it's about working together toward a healthier, stronger, and more connected relationship. Through experience, we've learned that every disagreement has an underlying cause, and when couples identify the real issue rather than seeing each

Understanding Conflict

other as the problem, conflict becomes a tool for growth rather than division.

Understanding conflict is the key to navigating disagreements effectively in marriage. Below are some practical tips that can help couples identify the root causes of conflict and approach them with patience, clarity, and teamwork. Conflicts should bring growth rather than division.

TIPS TO REMEMBER

1. Recognize That Conflict Is Normal

Many couples assume that frequent disagreements mean their relationship is failing, but conflict does not indicate a lack of love—it simply means two people have different perspectives. We must learn that disagreeing is natural, and handling it wisely is what makes a marriage stronger.

Tip: Reframe your mindset to see conflict as an opportunity for growth rather than a threat to the relationship. When approach correctly, challenges can lead to deeper understanding and stronger communication.

2. Identify the Root Cause

Before reacting emotionally, take a step back and ask: *What is the real issue here?* Sometimes, surface-level frustrations—like disagreements over chores, money, or plans—are actually rooted in deeper emotions such as stress, insecurity, or unmet expectations.

We must notice that arguments weren't always about what we thought they were about—sometimes external stress, exhaustion, or unresolved feelings influenced the way we communicate.

Tip: Before engaging in an argument, reflect on whether the frustration stems from the situation itself or external pressures influencing emotions. Identifying the true cause helps prevent unnecessary escalation.

3. Pause Before Reacting

In emotionally charged moments, the way we respond matters just as much as the issue itself. Pausing before reacting prevented misunderstandings. Many conflicts become worse simply because emotions take over before logic has time to process the situation.

Tip: Take a moment to breathe before responding, ensuring that your reaction is thoughtful rather than impulsive. If needed, briefly step away and revisit the conversation when both partners are calm.

4. Avoid Making Conflict Personal

A mistake many couples make is viewing their partner as the problem instead of identifying the actual issue. We must learn that financial stress isn't about us—it was about different money habits, and disagreements

Understanding Conflict

about daily routines that isn't about personal flaws—they are about differences in expectations.

Tip: Shift from blaming each other to collaborating on solutions. Instead of saying, *"You never listen,"* try **"**I feel unheard when this happens. Can we talk about how to fix it?" This keeps discussions solution-focused rather than emotionally charged.

5. Be Open to Compromise

Many conflicts happen because both partners want to feel heard but aren't open to adjusting their perspective. When we hold on to rigid positions without considering middle ground, discussions can become frustrating rather than productive.

Tip: Instead of focusing on who is right, shift the conversation to what solution works best for both partners. Compromise doesn't mean sacrificing values—it means finding a way to meet each other's needs without unnecessary resistance.

6. Understand That Conflict Often Has a History

Some disagreements feel bigger than they should because unresolved issues from the past resurface. When old frustrations appeared in new arguments, making resolution can be difficult.

Tip: Instead of letting past conflicts linger, make a conscious choice to resolve them fully. Don't carry previous frustrations into future discussions—address them, close the door, and move forward.

7. Use Conflict to Strengthen Connection

Conflict doesn't have to weaken a marriage—it can actually bring couples closer when handled with patience, respect, and teamwork. We must learn that when we approach disagreements with understanding, we can become more emotionally connected rather than divided.

Tip: After resolving an argument, take a moment to reaffirm your love for each other. A simple, *"I appreciate that we worked through that together"* reinforces emotional security and mutual respect.

By applying these tips, couples can turn conflict into an opportunity for deeper understanding rather than allowing it to create resentment. We must continue to embrace this mindset, ensuring that our love stays stronger than any disagreement we face.

30 Minutes Thursdays

Discussions Not Explainations

Every marriage encounter challenges—it's part of sharing life with another person. No matter how deep the love or strong the connection, two individuals with different experiences, personalities, and emotions will inevitably face disagreements. While conflict itself isn't the problem, how couples choose to handle it determines whether their relationship grows stronger or suffers from unresolved frustration.

Many couples struggle with conflict not because they don't love each other, but because they don't have a structured way to address disagreements without letting emotions take over. Some couples engage in heated discussions the moment frustration arises, often leading to unnecessary arguments that damage emotional intimacy. Others avoid conflict altogether, silently storing grievances until resentment builds. Neither approach fosters a healthy marriage.

This is why 30-Minute Thursdays offer a marriage-saving solution—giving couples dedicated time to discuss issues in a controlled, structured, and intentional way. Instead of letting frustrations dominate daily interactions or escalate into emotional disputes, couples commit to mentally bookmarking conflicts throughout the week and addressing them only during a designated 30-minute window.

By following this approach, couples shift from emotionally reactive conversations to calm, solution-focused discussions, protecting their relationship from negativity, tension, and unproductive cycles of blame. 30-Minute Thursdays aren't about avoiding conflict—they're about handling it strategically to strengthen love, unity, and mutual understanding.

Conflict is inevitable in relationships, but how couples manage disagreements determines whether their marriage thrives or weakens. Many couples assume that resolving disputes requires long, drawn-out conversations, but in reality, conflict doesn't need to take up unnecessary emotional space—it simply needs a system for resolution. 30-Minute Thursdays offer a structured approach that gives couples dedicated time to problem-solve without allowing emotions to take over or dragging minor frustrations into everyday interactions.

The concept is simple yet effective: instead of allowing disagreements to dictate the atmosphere of the relationship throughout the week, couples mentally bookmark issues that arise and commit to discussing them only during the designated 30-minute time slot. During this conversation, the focus is not on explaining why something happened, assigning blame, or rehashing frustrations—it's entirely about finding solutions and making adjustments to prevent the same issue from occurring again.

Thirty minutes is long enough to address concerns without dragging out negativity and short enough to keep discussions focused rather than exhausting. Also, it's a discussion not an argument. When couples set time limits on conflict discussions, it prevents endless cycles of frustration and ensures that issues are handled with clarity and purpose rather than emotional exhaustion.

This method prevents small conflicts from turning into ongoing tension, allowing couples to maintain peace in their marriage without having frequent emotional drain from unresolved frustrations. Rather than interrupting daily life with complaints, couples store concerns mentally and approach them strategically rather than reactively.

Every marriage, no matter how strong, will face conflict. It's a natural part of being in a relationship—two different people with unique backgrounds, expectations, and emotions coming together to build a life. While love is the foundation, how couples handle disagreements determines whether their marriage will thrive or crumble under the weight of unresolved frustrations.

Many couples unknowingly allow conflict to dominate their relationship, leading to tension, emotional exhaustion, and unnecessary strain. Some struggle because they try to address every issue immediately, often in heated moments, while others avoid discussing problems altogether, letting them pile up until resentment takes hold. Neither approach creates a healthy marriage.

This is where 30-Minute Thursdays come in—a structured, intentional method for addressing problems without letting them interfere with daily life. It's a simple but effective concept that allows couples to problem-solve together rather than argue emotionally, protecting their relationship and prioritizing love over frustration.

One of the mistakes couples make when managing conflict is keeping a record of every frustration—physically writing down grievances creates a mental "memory card," allowing resentment to build rather than fade. Kathleen and I quickly realized that when we constantly documented our complaints, we were reinforcing them rather than preparing to resolve them.

By keeping issues only as mental notes, couples ensure that if something truly matters, they'll remember it—but if it's minor, it will naturally fade away. This mental filtering process prevents unnecessary discussions about things that don't actually need resolution.

HOW DOES IT WORK?

Step 1: Bringing Up the Issue Without Emotion

When Thursday arrives (or any chosen day), couples begin by stating the problem clearly, without over-explaining or attaching emotion to it. This method helps eliminate defensive reactions and keeps the conversation focused.

For example:

- **Wrong Approach:** *"You were careless, and the glass broke! How many times have I told you to be more careful?"*
- **Right Approach:** *"The glass broke. How can we prevent this from happening again?"*

This shift removes blame and emotion, turning the conversation into a collaborative problem-solving session rather than an argument.

Step 2: Finding a Solution Together

Rather than debating what happened or explaining personal perspectives, couples must focus solely on how to prevent future occurrences.

For example:

- Instead of saying, *"You weren't watching what you were doing, and that's why the glass broke,"* say, *"Let's figure out a way to keep breakable objects in safer spots."*

The goal is not justification or blame—it's avoiding the same issue in the future.

Step 3: Handling Unresolved Topics

If couples cannot agree on a solution within the 30-minute timeframe or emotions begin interfering with discussion, they must move on to the next topic. This prevents cycles of frustration and allows space for reflection before revisiting the issue the following week.

Instead of forcing resolution in the moment, couples carry unresolved topics forward, ensuring discussions remain productive rather than emotionally overwhelming. Most arguments spiral into unnecessary emotional territory because couples spend more time discussing why the problem happened rather than how to fix it. This approach keeps conversations constructive, leading to quicker resolutions and less tension.

Holding frustrations until a scheduled day teaches patience, self-restraint, and emotional balance. Instead of reacting immediately, couples learn to think through their emotions before engaging in discussion, which leads to healthier conversations.

Many conflicts escalate because partners feel the need to defend themselves or explain why something happened. 30-Minute Thursdays eliminate this—it's not about explaining mistakes, it's about fixing them.

Many couples struggle with the impulse to address problems right away. Instead of engaging in immediate emotional reactions, remind yourself that the issue will be handled properly during the designated time.

The beauty of not writing issues down is that couples automatically filter out concerns that aren't truly important. If a topic slips the mind, it likely wasn't significant enough to discuss in the first place. If couples cannot reach an agreement within 30 minutes, the topic must be pushed to the next week, ensuring that frustration doesn't overwhelm the conversation.

By practicing 30-Minute Thursdays, couples develop emotional intelligence, patience, and intentionality, ensuring that conflict no longer controls the relationship—love does.

TIPS TO REMEMBER:

1. Commit to the Practice Weekly

Consistency is key—schedule 30-Minute Thursdays (or another preferred day) every single week. Treat it as a non-negotiable part of your relationship, just like date nights or family obligations. Make this time sacred for problem-solving, ensuring both partners are mentally prepared to engage productively.

2. Take Mental Notes, Not Written Records

Writing down grievances creates a "memory card" of complaints, which can lead to resentment and an unhealthy focus on problems. Instead, mentally store frustrations, allowing time and perspective to determine whether an issue is truly worth discussing. If a problem fades from memory, it probably wasn't significant enough to address in the first place.

3. Stay Solution-Oriented

When discussing an issue, avoid spending time explaining why it happened—this often leads to defensiveness, frustration, and emotional exhaustion. Instead, focus solely on problem-solving:

- *What can we do to prevent this issue from happening again?*
- *How can we adjust our approach moving forward?*

For example, if the glass of milk spills, there's no benefit in debating whose fault it was. Instead of saying, *"You were careless,"* or *"I wasn't paying attention, but I'll do better next time,"* shift to a problem-solving mindset: *"How can we avoid the glass of milk from spilling in the future?"*

4. Keep Emotions in Check

The purpose of 30-Minute Thursdays **is** problem-solving, not emotional venting. If one or both partners begin getting upset, acknowledge it and move on to the next topic. Allow space for reflection before readdressing unresolved issues the following week.

5. Set Boundaries Around Discussion Time

Stick to the 30-minute limit, no matter how many issues arise. This prevents conversations from becoming draining and overwhelming, ensuring conflict resolution stays efficient rather than emotionally exhausting. If an issue isn't solved, it carries over to the following week—but it does NOT dominate daily life.

6. Acknowledge Progress Rather Than Perfection

The goal of 30-Minute Thursdays is to work toward solutions and strengthen unity, not to achieve instant perfection. Kathleen and I found that even when some topics carried over to the next week, there was always progress in how we approached conversations, leading to healthier communication patterns over time.

7. Move Forward Instead of Dwelling on the Past

Focusing on why something happened or assigning blame will never rebuild emotional connection. A broken glass, forgotten task, or frustrating misunderstanding can't be undone—but future problems can be prevented. Embrace growth, adaptability, and teamwork, ensuring that each discussion serves a purpose in strengthening the relationship rather than draining it.

Couples must never allow arguments or unresolved disputes to dominate their marriage. 30-Minute Thursdays protect love by ensuring conflict resolution stays controlled, intentional, and solution-driven. Relationships flourish when problems are addressed efficiently, emotions are kept in check, and unity is prioritized above all else.

90/10 RULE

Condition The Mind to Be Poisitive

Kathleen and I have always believed that love is built—not just through grand gestures, but in the words we speak, the affirmations we share, and the way we navigate challenges with care. Relationships thrive when kindness and appreciation outweigh disagreements, which is why we've embraced the 90/10 rule: bathing 90% of our conversations with warmth, gratitude, and encouragement while reserving only 10% for concerns, disagreements, or disputes. This approach ensures that, no matter the conversation, we always leave each other with a sense of reassurance, love, and understanding.

90/10 Rule

Early in our relationship, we realized that the tone of our conversations mattered just as much as the words themselves. We often reflect on how good it feels when we celebrate each other's strengths—whether it is thanking your spouse for the way they support you during a tough day or sharing appreciates for the efforts made to keep put a smile on your face. These little moments become the foundation of your connection.

But, like every couple, we've had our moments of disagreement. There was a time when a small misunderstanding could lead to frustration, a single critical comment overshadowing an entire day of kindness. We saw how easy it was to let negativity take the lead, and we knew there had to be a better way. That's when we committed to making positivity our default, ensuring that every conversation left a lasting impression of love, not hurt.

The heart of the 90/10 rule is rooted in appreciation. One evening, after a long day, Kathleen surprised me with a heartfelt text: *"I just want you to know how much I appreciate everything you do. You bring me so much joy."* It was simple, but it made all the difference—it turned a stressful day into one filled with warmth. Then she said, *"don't forget to pick up milk, you always forget."*

Since then, we've made affirmations a daily practice. I tell Kathleen how much I admire her patience, how her laughter brightens my world. She reminds me that she believes in me, that she sees the good even when I doubt myself. We leave little notes for each other, saying things like, *"You're incredible"* or *"Thank you for always listening."* I would write love notes and place them in her underwear drawer, as she would to me when I am travelling and place them in my suitcase. Sometimes I would write notes on the bathroom mirror, draw a little rose and tell her how much I love her.

When we have conversations, we intentionally fill 90% of them with positive affirmations—celebrating each other, appreciating the little things, and reinforcing the love we share. Then, in the remaining 10%, we gently introduce concerns, ensuring they never dominate the warmth of our connection.

No matter what, we always end on a positive note, allowing the seeds of concern to settle naturally, rather than forcing explanations or turning them into heavy discussions. We trust that reflection will do its work, and we never let worries take up more space than the love we have for each other. Because at the heart of every conversation, love should always lead, rule, and remain stronger than any temporary frustration.

We strive for balance, but sometimes, one of us feels like we're carrying more of the load. One evening, Kathleen looked exhausted after doing most of the

90/10 Rule

housework and sighed, *"I feel like I do everything around here."*

Instead of jumping into a defensive explanation about how I contribute, I applied the 90/10 rule. I started with appreciation:

"You always make our home feel warm and welcoming. I love how much you care about creating a space that feels good for both of us."

Then, I gently introduced the concern:

"I noticed you always leave shoes by the front door."

We ended the conversation with positivity:

"I know we'll get this figured out. Let's have dinner together and relax."

By leading with appreciation and ending on a reassuring note, we avoided resentment and instead found a way to work together rather than against each other.

I enjoy going out and connecting with friends, while Kathleen prefers quieter nights at home. Sometimes, we don't align on weekend plans, which can lead to friction.

Instead of arguing when Kathleen expressed frustration—*"You always want to go places, and I just want a quiet night in."*—I shifted the conversation using the 90/10 rule.

90% affirmation: *"I love how much you find joy in our simple moments together. You make home feel like the best place to be."*

10% concern: *"I notice you always want to go places and get out of the house, instead of being with me."*

Ending with positivity: *"How can we come to some resolutions?*

Instead of making it a conflict, we turned the conversation into a solution, ensuring that both of our needs were met.

Money can be a sensitive topic, especially when partners have different spending habits. In the earlier days of our marriage, Kathleen enjoys occasional splurges, while I tend to be more financially cautious watching every penny spent.

One time, Kathleen bought something expensive without discussing it first. Instead of immediately questioning the purchase, I waited for a calm moment and framed the discussion using the 90/10 rule.

90% affirmation: *"I love how much joy you bring into life. You always find ways to make things special."*

10% concern: *"I noticed you spent quite a bit of money on the brand name clothes which I don't like."*

Ending with positivity: *"What can we do to balance our spending?"*

By reinforcing appreciation first, the conversation stayed constructive rather than tense.

Life gets busy—work, children, responsibilities—and sometimes, couples feel distant. Kathleen and I make an effort to keep intimacy a priority, but one day, she mentioned, *"I feel like we've been so busy, we haven't connected like we used to."*

Instead of feeling guilty or making excuses, I responded using the 90/10 rule.

90% affirmation: *"I love that you care about our connection. It's one of the things that makes our relationship so strong, being with each other."*

10% concern: *"I noticed our sex life is down the tubes, and you appear not to be interested."*

Ending with positivity: *"What can we do to create some sparks back into our sex life?"*

This approach ensured that instead of turning into blame or sadness, the conversation led to solutions that brought us closer. We started a monthly night away and weekly sushi date.

Stress can sometimes make couples unintentionally snap at each other. One day, Kathleen had a frustrating day and said something sharp—*"I feel like you're not even listening right now."*

Instead of reacting defensively, I let the comment sit. Later, when things were calm, Kathleen introduced the concern gently:

90% affirmation: *"I know you've had a tough day, and I love how strong you are even when things feel overwhelming."*

10% concern: *"I feel like you're not even listening right now, and I am speaking to the wall."*

Ending with positivity: *"What can we do to work on effective communication."*

This ensured the conversation didn't escalate, but instead became a moment of care and reflection.

Relationships flourish when love is always the priority, even in difficult discussions. By ensuring concerns never overshadow appreciation. Couples can keep discussions constructive rather than defensive, prevent resentment from building, reinforce mutual respect while still addressing important topics and end conversations feeling supported rather than attacked.

We've learned that appreciation doesn't have to wait for special occasions. It's in the way Kathleen compliments my cooking, even when I'm convinced it's just average. It's in how I tell her she looks beautiful, not because I think she needs to hear it, but because I genuinely mean it. These daily affirmations build a foundation of emotional security, creating a space where love is felt even in silence.

After any discussion—especially when there's disagreement—Kathleen and I make sure we end on a note of connection. No matter how tough a conversation might be, we close it with warmth. A simple, *"I love you"* or *"I'm grateful for us"* reminds us that our relationship is bigger than any temporary challenge.

One night, after a particularly frustrating day, I was venting about work. Kathleen listened, nodded, and offered support. Then, just as I was about to get lost in negativity, she gently squeezed my hand and said, *"Even on hard days, I hope you know how proud I am of you."* That single sentence shifted everything—I felt seen, appreciated, and reminded of the love we share.

One year, Kathleen and I planned a special anniversary dinner. We had talked about it for weeks—where we would go, what we would wear, how we'd make the evening unforgettable. But when the day arrived, I got caught up in work, lost track of time, and by the time I realized it, I was running late. Kathleen was disappointed. I could see it in her eyes—the day hadn't unfolded the way she imagined.

Instead of letting frustration take over, she took a breath and applied the 90/10 rule. Rather than dwelling on the fact that I was late, she started with appreciation: *"I know you've been working hard, and I love how*

That simple shift in how she framed her frustration made all the difference. I didn't feel attacked or blamed—I felt understood. And because she reinforced her appreciation for me first, I genuinely wanted to do better. I made an effort that day to clean up right away, and even after that, I became more mindful about keeping our shared space neat.

Kathleen and I don't always want the same thing when it come to how we spend our free time. One weekend, she was excited for a quiet night in—movies, snacks, just the two of us. But I had been looking forward to going out, socializing, and having some fun.

At first, we were stuck. I didn't want to stay home, and she wasn't feeling the energy for a night out. But instead of getting frustrated, we leaned into the 90/10 rule.

I smiled and said, *"I love how much you cherish our time together at home. You make even the simplest nights feel special."* Then, I added, *"But I also love when we go out and make memories beyond our little bubble. Maybe we can find a way to do both?"*

That shifted everything. Suddenly, it wasn't about choosing *my* idea or *her* idea—it was about finding something that honoured both of us. We compromised by going out for a little while and coming back early for a cozy evening together. That night ended up being one of our best because we were intentional about making it *dedicated you are to what you do. I just really [...] tonight to feel special for us."* She didn't att[...] blame—she expressed her feelings while still remi[...] me of what she valued about me.

Hearing her say that made me want to show up e[...] better. I admitted my mistake, apologized sincerely, a[...] we both focused on making the rest of the evenin[...] beautiful. Because Kathleen didn't lead with frustration[...] the night wasn't ruined. Instead, we ended up laughing, reminiscing, and celebrating what mattered most—our love.

Another example is Kathleen loves a clean kitchen. She says it helps her feel calm, like everything is in order. Me? I tend to leave a few dishes in the sink, promising I'll get to them later (though "later" sometimes turns into "tomorrow"). One afternoon, Kathleen walked into the kitchen and saw a pile of dishes I had left behind. She sighed—something about that mess just got under her skin.

Rather than instantly criticizing me, she remembered the 90/10 rule. She started with kindness: *"You know, one of the things I love about you is how relaxed and easygoing you are. It's one of the reasons being with you feels like home."* Then, she gently added, *"That being said, can we find a way to make sure the kitchen stays a little tidier? It really helps me feel more at peace."*

work for both of us rather than letting frustration take the lead.

We've faced plenty of moments where frustration *could* have taken over. But each time we practice the 90/10 rule—leading conversations with warmth, appreciation, and understanding—we build a stronger foundation.

It's not that challenges disappear, but they don't define the relationship. When appreciation outweighs frustration, even the tough conversations bring us closer.

Parenting is another example which can be one of the most delicate balancing acts in a marriage. We both want the best for our children, but sometimes our approaches differ. One evening, our son had broken a rule—nothing major, but enough to warrant a conversation. I was firm about consequences, believing structure was important, while Kathleen leaned toward a gentler approach.

Instead of letting frustration build, Kathleen softened the moment with appreciation: *"I love how much you care about teaching responsibility. It's one of the things that makes you such a great father."* That affirmation helped me listen rather than just react. In turn, I acknowledged her perspective: *"And I admire how much you prioritize understanding their emotions."*

With mutual respect leading the conversation, we arrived at a middle ground—balancing discipline with empathy. Because of the 90/10 rule, our son didn't just learn a lesson, but also witnessed what healthy communication looks like in marriage.

I've always been driven, pouring myself into work with full force. But sometimes, that means I struggle to step away—even when Kathleen needed me.

One night, she was excited to spend time together, but I was buried in emails. She could have expressed her frustration directly, but instead, she applied the 90/10 rule: *"I love how passionate you are about what you do. Your dedication is inspiring. But sometimes, I really miss you. Can we carve out some time to just be together tonight?"*

Hearing appreciation before concern made me realize how much my presence mattered. Without guilt or defensiveness clouding the moment, I shut my laptop, took her hand, and we enjoyed an evening where nothing else mattered but us.

Life gets chaotic—between work, parenting, responsibilities, and commitments, finding time for romance isn't always easy. We've fallen into a cycle where date nights kept getting postponed.

Instead of letting it turn into resentment, we approached it with the 90/10 rule. I started by acknowledging her effort: *"I love that you always make time for us, even when life is overwhelming. Our time together means everything to me."* She responded with warmth: *"And I love how much you make me laugh. No matter how busy things get, I never stop appreciating the joy you bring."*

By leading with gratitude, we turned the conversation into an opportunity rather than an issue. That night, we set a standing monthly date—something that always gave us moments to look forward to, strengthening our connection in the midst of life's chaos.

Every couple navigates the delicate balance of privacy—what to share with family and friends, and what to protect as sacred between us.

We've had different perspectives on this. I often spoke openly about personal matters with my family, while Kathleen preferred keeping things private. When she felt uneasy about something I had shared, instead of reacting negatively, she used the 90/10 approach: *"I love how close you are with your family. I admire the trust you have with them. But sometimes, I'd love for certain moments to just be ours."*

Her words weren't restrictive, they were reassuring. I listened, adjusted, and we found a middle ground—choosing what moments deserved to be ours alone and which ones were meant to be shared.

90/10 Rule

I tend to be meticulous when it comes to keeping the house spotless. Kathleen, while she appreciates a clean space, doesn't experience the same urgency I do.

One day, after tidying up obsessively, I found myself frustrated that she didn't see it as the same priority. But instead of criticizing, I caught myself and shifted gears: *"I love how relaxed you are—it's part of what balances me. I also know I have certain habits that aren't yours, and I never want them to feel like pressure on you."*

She responded with warmth: *"And I love how much you care. I'll try to be more mindful, but I appreciate that you don't expect me to see things exactly the way you do."*

That understanding helped us create harmony without turning cleaning into tension.

Investing in a rental property in Erin, Ontario was something I felt strongly about. I saw the potential, ran the numbers, and believed it could be a smart move for our future. But Kathleen wasn't as convinced—she worried about risk, about the strain it could put on our finances, and about whether it would be worth it in the long run.

At first, I struggled with guilt, feeling like I was pushing for something she didn't fully agree with. But instead of letting that guilt sit between us, we applied the 90/10 rule.

Kathleen started the conversation with warmth: *"I admire how forward-thinking you are, how much you care about securing our future. I love how you dream big."*

That made me feel understood rather than dismissed. I responded with my own affirmation: *"And I respect your ability to think critically and protect us from unnecessary risks."*

That mutual validation helped us move forward—not by forcing an agreement, but by ensuring that whatever decision we made, we made it together. The conversation ended with reassurance rather than tension, and in the end, we found a way to move forward with clarity and unity.

I've always had a hard time saying no. Whether it's work, family, or helping a friend, I naturally take on too much. Eventually, it catches up with me, leaving me drained.

One evening, Kathleen noticed I was exhausted—overcommitted, stretched too thin. Instead of telling me outright that I was overdoing it, she led with kindness: *"I love how generous you are with your time. You always go above and beyond for people. But I also want to make sure you're taking care of yourself too."*

That softened the message. Instead of feeling defensive, I felt cared for. It allowed me to open up about the struggle I had with saying no, and in turn, Kathleen encouraged me to set healthier boundaries. The conversation became an opportunity for support rather than criticism, and from then on, I started being more mindful about protecting my own energy.

Our families approach communication and support very differently. My family has always been open, transparent, and involved, while Kathleen's family tends to be more private and reserved. Sometimes, this difference creates challenges—Kathleen might feel overwhelmed by how open my family is, and I might struggle to understand why her family holds back.

Instead of letting this difference become a source of resentment, we apply the 90/10 rule.

One evening, Kathleen expressed her thoughts warmly: *"I love how deeply connected you are with your family. The way you support each other is beautiful. But sometimes, I feel like I need more space when it comes to sharing certain things."*

Because she framed her concern with appreciation, I didn't feel like she was rejecting my family's openness—I understood that she was expressing her own emotional needs. I responded with mutual affirmation: *"I respect how thoughtful you are about boundaries. I want to make sure we handle our family dynamics in a way that feels right for both of us."*

That conversation allowed us to navigate our cultural differences with understanding rather than frustration, finding middle ground that honored both our perspectives.

I've always been conscious of health—what I eat, how often I exercise, and how I take care of myself. As we get older, I feel it's even more important to prioritize these habits. Kathleen, on the other hand, doesn't see it as much of a necessity. She enjoys life without overthinking food choices or strict workout routines, which can sometimes make it difficult for us to align.

One day, I found myself hesitating to bring up fitness again, afraid she might see it as me pressuring her. Instead, I used the 90/10 rule and approached the conversation gently:

"I love how much you embrace life fully. You have an ease and joy that I deeply admire. At the same time, I also want to make sure we take care of our health so we can enjoy life together for as long as possible."

Kathleen smiled, appreciating the sentiment rather than feeling criticized. She responded with warmth: *"And I love that you care so much about us. I might not always approach health the way you do, but I respect the way you prioritize it."*

That moment reinforced that while our approaches might be different, our goals are the same. We both want to live long, healthy lives together, and that mutual understanding helped us bridge the gap.

I'm someone who has no problem asking for help when I need it—Kathleen, on the other hand, finds it difficult. Whether it's needing support with a task, expressing emotional struggles, or simply leaning on others, she's used to handling things on her own.

One evening, she seemed overwhelmed with work, but she didn't ask for help. I wanted to offer support without making her feel pressured, so I used the 90/10 rule.

"I love how independent and capable you are. You take on so much and handle it with grace. But I also want you to know that you don't have to do everything alone—I'm always here to support you."

Kathleen softened, realizing that my words weren't about questioning her ability, but reminding her that she wasn't alone. Instead of brushing off the stress, she accepted my help that evening, and from then on, she became more open to receiving support when she needed it.

Each of these moments proves that relationships thrive when we approach challenges with warmth, appreciation, and mutual respect. The 90/10 rule doesn't mean ignoring difficulties—it means addressing them in a way that preserves love rather than damages it.

By leading conversations with kindness, Kathleen and I transform everyday struggles into deeper connection. No matter what the challenge—whether it's managing family dynamics, discussing financial decisions, setting boundaries, or navigating intimacy—we always ensure that love remains the foundation of every exchange.

Because at the end of the day, it's not about avoiding conflict—it's about making sure that every conversation strengthens, rather than weakens, what we've built together. Couple faces unique challenges, and relationships evolve through the way partners handle them. Every relationship faces challenges—differences in personality, perspectives, habits, and priorities. But what makes love last is how couples handle those challenges.

The 90/10 rule ensures that love always outweighs frustration, and that even difficult conversations lead to understanding rather than division. Kathleen and I have learned that kindness isn't just about grand gestures—it's woven into the everyday words we speak.

No matter what the scenario—whether it's navigating stress, managing responsibilities, aligning personal goals, or simply handling daily disagreements—the way we talk to each other determines how strong our bond remains. And in the end, the greatest gift any couple can give each other is the reassurance that love is always stronger than conflict.

TIPS TO REMEMBER:

1. Start Conversations with Gratitude

Before expressing a concern, begin with an affirmation. Instead of saying, *"You never listen to me,"* try *"I love how much you care about me—I just want to feel heard in this moment."* This sets a positive tone and helps avoid defensiveness.

2. Make Appreciation a Daily Habit

Don't wait for special occasions—express gratitude often. Whether it's a simple *"I love how thoughtful you are"* or *"Thank you for making me laugh today,"* small affirmations build emotional security.

3. Frame Criticism Gently

When addressing an issue, avoid making it feel like an attack. Instead of *"You never help with the dishes,"* say *"I appreciate how much you do for us. I'd love if we could find a way to share the workload more evenly."* This keeps the conversation constructive rather than confrontational.

4. Leave Conversations on a Positive Note

Even when discussing disagreements, close with warmth. Saying *"No matter what, I love you"* ensures that even difficult talks end with reassurance.

5. Avoid Keeping Score

Relationships aren't about winning arguments or keeping track of who does more. Focus on collaboration rather than competition, ensuring both partners feel valued.

6. Create Rituals for Connection

Set up small but meaningful habits—whether it's sharing daily appreciations, setting intentional date nights, or ending the day with a positive reflection about each other.

7. Know When to Pause

If a discussion is getting too heated, take a break before saying something regretful. Give each other space, then return with a mindset focused on resolution rather than frustration.

8. Reframe Conflict as a Team Effort

Rather than seeing disagreements as *me vs. you*, think of it as *us vs. the problem*. Shifting the mindset helps couples approach challenges with unity rather than division.

9. Understand Each Other's Love Languages

People receive love differently—through words, gestures, quality time, or physical affection. Know how your partner feels most appreciated and make it a priority.

10. Condition the Mind to Focus on Strengths

Make a habit of mentally listing what you love about your partner, especially in moments of frustration. Training your mind to highlight the positives ensures your relationship remains rooted in appreciation rather than criticism.

Relationships are shaped by the thoughts we nurture. If we focus only on the negatives, even the most beautiful love can feel distant. We've trained ourselves to look for the positives—to remind ourselves daily that there is far more good between us than bad. Every couple faces challenges. But the way we navigate them—the way we choose to elevate love over frustration—makes all the difference. By bathing our conversations in kindness, appreciation, and understanding, we strengthen the connection that holds us together. Because in the end, love isn't measured by the absence of conflict—it's measured by how much warmth remains, even when disagreements arise. And for Kathleen and me, that warmth is always there, growing stronger with every conversation.

PLANTING THE SEED

Opportunity For Growth

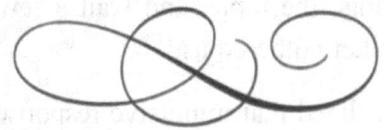

Kathleen and I have learned that conflict, disputes, and disagreements are inevitable in any relationship. But the way we respond to them can make the difference between emotional scars and growth. Early on, we realized that impulsive reactions can escalate situations beyond what is necessary—like someone throwing a ball at you, and instead of dropping it, you immediately throw it back, with force. Or when someone takes a swing at you, your natural response is to block, defend, or counter the attack.

Verbal exchanges can feel the same way. When a partner says something hurtful, it's easy to react in the moment—throwing words back like weapons, cutting each other down. But Kathleen and I didn't want that kind of relationship. We wanted to eliminate emotional abuse, avoid lasting wounds, and ensure that even in disagreement, our love remained the foundation of our communication.

That's when we embraced the idea of *Planting the Seed*—a method where we pause, let emotions settle, and then revisit concerns once the dust has settled. Sometimes, we'll leave an issue for 30 minutes Thursday (a designated time for addressing small disputes), other times we'll apply the 90/10 rule, or we simply bite our tongues, change the topic, and wait a few days before expressing what bothered us.

We've realized that impulsive responses rarely lead to resolution—they just lead to deeper frustration. But when you plant a seed, you introduce the thought gently, letting it take root without forcing an immediate explanation or defense.

One evening, Kathleen and I had a small argument—one of those moments where words slipped out in frustration. She told me, *"You never listen."* Those words stung. My instinct was to immediately jump in with *"Of course I listen! That's not fair."* But I caught myself—I knew that reacting defensively would only push us further into a back-and-forth that wouldn't resolve anything.

Instead, I paused. I let the comment linger, but I didn't let it consume me. A few days later, when things were calm, I casually said, *"The other day, when you said I never listen, that bothered me. But, needless to say, that was a few days ago."*

Kathleen started to explain—she wanted to justify why she said it. But I did not allow her to explain, because if she explained then the seed planted would be cancelled. She would not have nothing to think about. Instead, I lightly changed the topic.

"What are we having for dinner?" "Let's grab a coffee." "I love you."

With that, the thought remained in her mind—but without the pressure of confrontation. The seed was planted. She had time to reflect, to sit with it, and to acknowledge it on her own terms. And the chances of her saying those words again? Minimal.

Unless, of course, the intent was vindictive—but that's a different conversation.

We've come to understand that words can either build or break trust. Some phrases, spoken in anger, can linger long after the argument is forgotten. That's why emotional regulation is so critical. When we resist the urge to react immediately, we gain clarity—not just in what we want to say, but in how we want our relationship to feel.

It's easy to let small frustrations snowball—like when we navigate parenting decisions, discuss finances, or even decide how to split household responsibilities. But when we take a step back, we realize that most conflicts don't need immediate confrontation.

Take parenting, for example. One day, Kathleen and I had differing views on how to handle a situation with our son. She wanted to be more lenient, while I believed a firmer approach was necessary. Instead of jumping into a heated argument, we let the moment pass allow the dust to settle. A few days later, I subtly introduced the topic:

"The other day, I felt like I wanted to be stricter with our son for his behaviour, but needless to say, that was a few days ago."

No pressure. No forcing a debate. Just planting the seed. That allowed Kathleen to reflect—not defensively, but thoughtfully. I told her she does not need to explain why she dismissed me during the discussion of my addressing our son.

One of the biggest mistakes couples make is demanding an explanation for every hurtful comment. If your partner says something harsh, your immediate instinct might be to ask, *"Why did you say that?"* or *"Explain yourself."* But that only leads to justification, excuses, and possibly more frustration.

The goal of *Planting the Seed* is to introduce the concern without reopening the wound. It's about letting them sit with it, ponder it, and hopefully self-correct over time.

Take our experience with social preferences. I'm more outgoing, while Kathleen prefers quiet nights in. There was a time when I pushed for more social events, not realizing she was feeling overwhelmed. One night, in exhaustion, she said, *"You always make plans without thinking about whether I want to go."*

Ouch. I could have defended myself right away, but instead, I waited. A few days later, I said casually:

"The other day, when you said I always make plans without thinking about whether you want to go —that bothered me. You know I always ask if you want to join me. But, needless to say, that was a few days ago."

As Kathleen started to explain, but I redirected: *"No worries. What movie should we watch tonight?"*

That seed stayed with her. From then on, she knew I cared about her social boundaries—without me needing to fight her over the comment.

Not every partner will reflect on the seeds you plant. Some will repeat the hurtful words intentionally, testing whether they can manipulate or push emotional limits. That's when it's important to recognize whether a comment was made out of frustration or out of cruelty.

If Kathleen and I ever feel like an issue is intentionally repetitive, we address it in a different way—not through planting the seed, but through direct discussion on our 30 minutes Thursdays.

Thankfully, our relationship thrives on mutual respect. Most of the time, the seed takes root naturally, making sure small conflicts never become lasting emotional wounds.

Kathleen and I know that love isn't about avoiding conflict—it's about handling it in a way that strengthens, rather than weakens, our connection.

By planting seeds instead of throwing verbal punches, we allow time for reflection. We trust that our words, once spoken with clarity, will resonate without the need for forced resolution.

We both value family, but sometimes, our expectations for how much time we spend with extended relatives don't align. I grew up in a household where frequent family gatherings were the norm, while Kathleen's family tends to be more private.

One weekend, I planned a visit to my parents without checking if Kathleen wanted to join. She sighed and said, *"You don't always think about whether I want to go or not."*

Instead of reacting defensively in the moment, I planted the seed a few days later:

"The other day, when you said I don't always consider whether you want to visit my family, that bothered me. But, needless to say, it was a few days ago."

Kathleen started to explain her perspective, but I smoothly redirected the conversation: *"What do you want to do for dinner tonight?"*

That left her with time to reflect on her words without pressure, and moving forward, we became more intentional about planning family time together in a way that felt right for both of us.

And that is the heart of our relationship—not perfection, but a continuous effort to communicate in ways that strengthen rather than damage the connection we've built.

After a busy week, Kathleen had been handling most of the household chores while I was caught up with work. One evening, she sighed loudly while cleaning, then muttered, *"I always end up doing everything."*

I could have immediately responded with, *"That's not true! I help out a lot!"* But I knew that would lead to a defensive back-and-forth. Instead, I let the moment pass.

A few days later, I planted the seed:

Planting The Seed

"The other day, when you said you always end up doing everything, that stuck with me. But, needless to say, it was a few days ago."

As she started to explain her frustration, but I redirected: *"Want to grab a coffee?"*

That gentle nudge helped her recognize the imbalance without an argument. In the following weeks, I noticed she was more open when asking for help, and I also made sure to step up more—without resentment lingering.

I've always been health-conscious—watching what I eat, exercising regularly, and prioritizing well-being. Kathleen, while supportive, doesn't feel the same urgency about fitness.

One evening, after I came back from the gym, Kathleen casually said, *"You make such a big deal out of working out. It's not like we need to go so hard at our age."*

I could have argued right then—telling her how much fitness mattered to me or that I wasn't making a "big deal." But I let it go.

A few days later, I gently planted the seed: *"The other day, when you said I make a big deal out of working out, that bothered me. But, needless to say, it was a few days ago."*

Kathleen started to clarify her words, but I smoothly shifted: Finances can be a tricky subject for couples, especially when one partner is more frugal and the other enjoys occasional splurges.

I've been hesitant about unnecessary purchases, while Kathleen enjoys treating herself and creating joy through small indulgences.

One day, Kathleen bought an expensive item without discussing it first. I instinctively wanted to question the choice, but instead of bringing it up immediately, I waited until later in the week to plant the seed:

"Hey honey, the other day, when I saw the purchase, I felt uneasy, I wished you had discussed it with me before. But, needless to say, that was a few days ago."

As soon as Kathleen started to explain why she bought it, but I redirected: *"No worries. Want to grab a coffee?"*

That left space for her to reflect. The next time she wanted to make a big purchase, she naturally checked in with me first—not because I forced her to, but because she subconsciously became more mindful of our shared financial goals.

In long-term relationships, it's easy to get caught up in routines and forget to appreciate the little things. Kathleen and I make a strong effort to express gratitude,

Planting The Seed

but even then, there are moments when one of us feels unnoticed.

One evening, Kathleen had gone out of her way to help organize something for me, and I had been so focused on work that I barely acknowledged it. Later, she sighed and quietly said, *"I don't even think you noticed what I did, no appreciations for what I did."*

Instead of responding right then and there, I let the moment pass. A few days later, I casually planted the seed:

"The other day, when you said I didn't notice what you did, that bothered me. You could have asked how my day was. But, needless to say, that was a few days ago."

Kathleen was about to explain, but I shifted the conversation with warmth: *"I know you are busy as well and do appreciate you. Let's grab dinner."*

That message sat with her. And going forward, I made an even greater effort to acknowledge her actions, ensuring she never felt overlooked again.

Couples often fall into habits where one person feels like they take on more of the daily chores or errands. Kathleen and I always aim to maintain balance, but sometimes, one of us might feel like the workload isn't evenly distributed.

One afternoon, after a busy week, I vented my frustration: *"I feel like I do so much, and it's exhausting."*

In that moment, she could have countered with her own perspective—she handles other tasks, work long hours, contribute in different ways. But instead of reacting immediately, she let my words sit.

Later in the week, she gently planted the seed:

"The other day, when you said you felt exhausted from doing too much, that was not an accurate statement. But, needless to say, that was a few days ago."

As I started to explain, she changed the topic: *"We both work long hours. What movie should we watch tonight?"*

That reflection helped me be more mindful, ensuring I proactively stepped in to share responsibilities without feeling like it had to be a debated conversation.

Even in close relationships, partners need personal space. Kathleen and I love spending time together, but we also value moments of independence.

One weekend, I had been eager to plan time together, while Kathleen had been craving alone time to read, relax, and recharge. At one point, she said, *"I feel like I don't get enough time to myself."*

I could have responded defensively, saying I wasn't trying to take away her personal time. But instead, I let her words settle. A few days later, I casually planted the seed:

"The other day, when you said you don't get enough alone time, which lingered with me. But, needless to say, that was a few days ago."

As she started to clarify, I lightly transitioned: *"Want to go for a walk?"*

From that point forward, I made a conscious effort to recognize when Kathleen needed space, ensuring she felt supported in her moments of solitude.

Sometimes, conflicts arise not from what is said, but how it's said. Kathleen and I have both had moments where the tone of voice led to unintended frustration.

One day, in a rushed conversation, I answered Kathleen's question with a short, distracted response. She immediately reacted: *"You sounded annoyed when you said that."*

I could have instantly defended myself—arguing that I wasn't annoyed, just preoccupied—but instead, I let the moment pass.

A few days later, I gently introduced the thought:

"The other day, when you said my tone sounded annoyed, that stuck with me. But, needless to say, that was a few days ago."

As Kathleen started to explain, I redirected: *"your look amazing today, I was thinking I should cook something fun tonight."*

That helped her reflect—not as a reaction, but as a realization. From then on, whenever we noticed tension in tone, we both approached it more mindfully.

Planting the seed isn't about avoiding conflict—it's about handling concerns in a way that allows reflection rather than defensiveness. Kathleen and I have learned that timing, emotional regulation, and intentional phrasing make all the difference in how issues are resolved.

By introducing concerns gently and letting them settle in the subconscious rather than demanding immediate justification, we eliminate unnecessary arguments, ensuring that love always outweighs frustration.

TIPS TO REMEMBER:

1. Pause Before Reacting

- When something bothers you, resist the urge to respond immediately. Take a breath, let emotions settle, and remind yourself that impulsive reactions rarely lead to resolution.
- If necessary, excuse yourself from the situation—go for a walk, shift your focus to

Planting The Seed

something else, and allow your emotions to regulate.

2. Choose the Right Moment

- Timing is everything. Instead of addressing an issue when tensions are high, wait a few hours or even a few days until the atmosphere is calm.
- Look for a neutral, relaxed setting—perhaps over coffee or during a casual conversation, when both of you feel emotionally open.

3. Frame It as a Passing Thought

- When bringing up something that bothered you, don't make it the centerpiece of the conversation. Instead, slip it in casually:
  - *"The other day, when you said I never listen, that stuck with me. But, needless to say, that was a few days ago."*
- By presenting it subtly, your partner is more likely to reflect rather than react defensively.

4. Redirect the Conversation

- Immediately after planting the seed, change the subject to something lighthearted or unrelated. This prevents the other person from explaining or justifying what they said, ensuring the thought remains in their mind.

- Examples:
  - *"Anyway, what are we having for dinner?"*
  - *"Let's grab a coffee."*
  - *"I love you."*

5. Trust the Reflection Process

- When you plant the seed, trust that your partner will think about it in their own time rather than forcing an immediate resolution.
- If the comment was made out of frustration rather than malice, your partner will likely self-correct moving forward.

6. Recognize Patterns & Set Boundaries

- If the same issue repeatedly arises, assess whether the behavior is accidental or intentional.
- If your partner continually dismisses your concerns, a direct conversation may be needed to prevent recurring emotional wounds.

7. Avoid Over-Explaining or Seeking Justification

- The goal isn't to rehash the conflict—it's to drop a thought into their subconscious and let it work naturally.
- Avoid asking, *"Why did you say that?"* or *"Can you explain?"* This opens the door for

rationalizations, which might cancel the effectiveness of the seed.

8. Show Consistent Positivity

- Even when addressing uncomfortable topics, reinforce the foundation of love by ensuring that most of your conversations remain positive.
- Express appreciation and affection before and after planting the seed, preventing resentment from building.

By applying these techniques, you create an emotionally intelligent way to navigate relationship challenges, ensuring concerns are acknowledged without unnecessary conflict.

- Resist the impulse to respond emotionally. Let the moment pass.
- Wait until emotions settle before bringing up what bothered you.
- Introduce the concern subtly, without making it a focal point.
- Change the topic immediately to prevent justification or defensiveness.
- Trust that reflection will do the work naturally—without forcing a conversation.

This method allows couples to navigate conflict with emotional intelligence, reducing arguments while fostering understanding. It's not about ignoring concerns—it's about handling them in a way that ensures change without resentment.

Planting The Seed

SHOCK THE BRAIN

Change Your Thinking

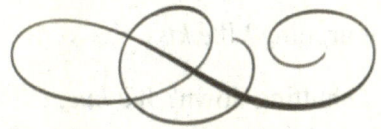

Love flourishes when partners respect each other's emotional needs. Some disagreements require space—time to process before diving into resolution. We all have learned that forcing conversations in the wrong moment can make things worse. If emotions are running high, we don't push for resolution right away. We give each other time—sometimes a few hours, sometimes longer—before revisiting the conversation with a calmer perspective.

Some discussions are best saved for private moments. If we're around others and tension surfaces, we agree to pause and come back to the discussion later, ensuring that external pressures don't worsen the disagreement. We've realized that timing makes all the difference. Instead of tackling tough conversations when exhausted, distracted, or overwhelmed, we choose moments when we can be fully present—ensuring clarity, not chaos.

One powerful lesson we've learned is that sometimes, the best response to frustration is doing the opposite of what comes naturally. When tension is rising, the brain expects defensive words, withdrawal, or irritation. But instead of feeding into those impulses, we interrupt them—shocking the brain by responding with love instead.

Instead of arguing? *We kiss.*

Instead of shutting down? *We hug.*

Instead of feeding negativity? *We make a joke, laugh, and shift the energy.*

One time, we were on the verge of an argument about something small—an oversight, a miscommunication, nothing that should have mattered in the long run. But it felt frustrating in the moment.

Instead of saying something sharp, I walked up to her, kissed her on the forehead, and smiled.

She stared at me, confused for half a second—and then burst into laughter.

Suddenly, the argument disappeared. Love took over.

This approach isn't about ignoring concerns—it's about choosing connection first, ensuring that love always has the final word.

A happy relationship isn't built on never experiencing conflict—it's built on choosing love over frustration, time over impulsivity, and connection over control.

- We use a secret word to defuse tension in public.
- We give each other space and set boundaries to handle conflicts with clarity.
- We shock the brain by responding with love instead of aggression.

These small habits create big emotional safety, ensuring that even in frustration, love remains our foundation. Because in the end, arguments come and go—but choosing each other, every single time, is what makes love last.

For example, there was a time we were out with friends and Kathleen misunderstood something I said. She shot me a look—the kind that clearly meant, *"We'll be talking about this later."* I could feel the frustration brewing, but instead of letting it turn into awkward silence or passive aggression, I leaned in and whispered our secret word.

Kathleen laughed. Instantly, the energy shifted. We weren't ignoring the issue—we were simply postponing it, ensuring that conflict didn't rule the moment.

Using a secret word is like a reset button—a reminder that the argument can wait, but love should always be present.

Love isn't about avoiding conflict—it's about keeping it from taking control. Relationships thrive when partners choose connection over frustration, and sometimes, that means getting creative in how we handle disagreements. Over time, we've discovered simple strategies that help us interrupt negativity, ease tension, and redirect emotions before they spiral.

One evening, we had a disagreement about finances. The conversation was getting tense, and neither of us was willing to back down. Instead of continuing to push our points in frustration, we agreed:

"Let's take a break from this conversation and revisit it tomorrow when we both feel clearer."

The next day, when we picked the conversation back up, the tension was gone, and instead of arguing, we worked together to find solutions.

Every couple has recurring disagreements—topics that seem to create friction again and again. Instead of letting these conflicts take over, we must create clear boundaries about when and how we address difficult subjects.

- It ensures big conversations happen at the right time—not when emotions are unpredictable.
- It protects social settings, family gatherings, and public moments from unnecessary tension.
- It prevents partners from associating love with constant conflict, ensuring the relationship remains emotionally safe.

At one point, we realized we were having heated conversations about parenting while we were in front of the kids. We agreed on a boundary: No serious parenting discussions when we're actively around them. Instead, we set aside time in private—when we could discuss things openly without the pressure of the moment. This boundary helped us maintain emotional safety at home, ensuring our children never felt caught in the middle of tension.

Shocking the brain is to choose love over impulsivity. Perhaps one of the most transformative strategies we have embraced is doing the opposite of what frustration tells us to do.

When couples face conflict, the natural impulse is often:

- To argue back.

- To shut down.
- To withdraw emotionally.

But instead of giving frustration control, we interrupt the pattern by choosing connection over conflict.

- It shifts the energy instantly, keeping love present even in difficult moments.
- It reinforces that love is bigger than disagreements.
- It allows partners to override emotional triggers and act intentionally instead of impulsively.

One time, Kathleen and I were both having a stressful week. We were short with each other, misinterpreting tones, and generally not feeling connected. At one point, during what could have turned into a heated exchange, I paused, leaned in, and hugged Kathleen instead of responding defensively.

She looked at me, confused for a moment—and then smiled. The tension disappeared instantly. Instead of pushing the argument, we ended up laughing, reconnecting, and realizing neither of us actually wanted to fight—we just needed reassurance.

No argument should ever threaten the strengths of your relationship. Because love should rule and reign—not frustration, not bitterness, and certainly not separation

After a long day, Kathleen and I sometimes approach the evening differently. I might still have energy to talk, catch up, or do something engaging, while Kathleen might need quiet, relaxation, and space to unwind.

One night, I excitedly started sharing details about a concern I had, but Kathleen, exhausted, sighed and said, *"I just don't have the energy for this right now, she kissed me and went to bed."*

I could have taken it personally—felt dismissed, assumed she didn't want to hear me out—but instead, I bit my tongue and gave her space, kissed her and walked to the washroom and allow my emotions to be expressed without anyone hearing me. I've learned not to show my weaknesses as no once resolve how I feel.

That moment allowed Kathleen to rest her thoughts and not feel obligated to have a conversion when she is not prepared for it.

Relationships don't survive because couples never argue—they survive because love consistently outweighs conflict. By giving space, setting boundaries, and interrupting negativity with love, we ensure that no disagreement ever threatens what we've built together.

Because love should always rule and reign—not frustration, not bitterness, and certainly not separation.

There are moments when frustration surfaces—maybe we're with friends, in public, or even mid-conversation at a family gathering. In these instances, it's not always appropriate (or productive) to engage in a heated exchange. We have a secret word—something lighthearted, something personal, something that instantly reminds us to pause, breathe, and reset.

If tension begins to rise, one of us subtly slips our secret word into the conversation, and just like that, it changes the tone. It shocks the brain from thinking we will be arguing to maintaining a peace.

Love flourishes in a peaceful, emotionally safe environment. That doesn't mean avoiding disagreements—it means handling them with care, emotional intelligence, and a commitment to staying connected even in frustration.

Instead of forcing a conversation when emotions are raw, space allows both partners to process feelings before returning to a discussion with level-headedness. It prevents conversations from turning into heated exchanges or hurtful words that linger. It reinforces that stepping away isn't abandoning the conversation—it's prioritizing emotional well-being.

Sometimes, the most productive way to handle conflict is to step away from it. When emotions are heightened, and frustration clouds rational thinking, hence giving each other space allows for clarity.

Conflict itself isn't the cause of emotional separation, breakups, or divorce—it's how couples handle conflict that determines whether a relationship grows stronger or weakens.

Love should always have the final word in conflict. Interrupt negativity with affection, humor, or kindness. Relationships don't break because of disagreements—they break when love is overshadowed by unresolved frustration, recurring negativity, and emotional neglect. By choosing to handle conflict, space is needed, intentional boundaries are a must, emotional safety and allowing love to override impulsivity.

And in the end, relationships aren't built on winning arguments. They're built on mutual respect, emotional intelligence, and ensuring that the words we choose always lead to healing, never destruction.

CHOOSING BATTLES WISELY

Is the Argument Worth It?

Not all conflicts need to turn into heated arguments. One of the most important lessons we have learned in our marriage is to ask ourselves whether the disagreement is truly worth the emotional toll it could take. If the argument is over something minor—like how to fold laundry or which restaurant to choose—we take a step back and decide whether it's worth disrupting peace over it.

Stress can make small disagreements feel bigger than they really were. Choosing which discussions truly

Choosing Battles Wisely

matter has helped us avoid unnecessary tension and protect our emotional bond.

Conflict in marriage is inevitable, but how couples choose to approach disagreements determines the strength of their relationship. Every couple will face challenges, whether it's differences in personality, upbringing, habits, or emotional expression. Not all battles are worth fighting, and some conflicts are best handled with understanding and compromise rather than prolonged disputes. Learning to choose battles wisely has helped us protect the peace in our marriage and foster deeper emotional connection.

Early in our marriage, we found ourselves getting caught up in minor frustrations that, in the grand scheme of things, weren't worth the stress they caused. One such moment was over how to organize our kitchen. I had a clear system for where everything should go, while Kathleen was more flexible in her approach. At first, she didn't understand why it mattered so much to me, and I couldn't see why she didn't naturally follow my system. It led to unnecessary tension, until we stepped back and asked ourselves—*Is this disagreement worth disrupting the peace in our home?* The answer was clear—it wasn't. We realized that our connection was more valuable than proving a point, and simply adjusting to accommodate each other was far easier than continuing the debate.

In the early days of our marriage, Kathleen noticed that I liked everything in its designated place, and any shift from that order created frustration. At first, she resisted this, feeling like it was unnecessary to be so particular about small household details. But as time passed, she realized that organization made me feel comfortable and in control, while her relaxed approach made herself feel less pressured. Instead of turning it into a daily conflict, we compromised—I maintained my structured system for important areas of the house, and Kathleen kept her flexibility in spaces that didn't affect my routine. This allowed us both to feel respected while avoiding needless arguments.

One of the first lessons we learned was that not every disagreement needs to escalate into an argument. When couples first get married, they often believe that they must tackle every issue head-on, but research suggests that successfully navigating conflict is about prioritization rather than confrontation (Johnson & Green, 2020). If we spend energy arguing over every small thing, we would constantly be drained and disconnected. Instead, focused on identifying which discussions were truly necessary and which ones you could simply let go.

Choosing battles wisely also applies to handling differences in emotional reactions. Kathleen processes emotions outwardly, preferring to talk through concerns, while I internalize before speaking. This difference sometimes led to frustration—she felt like I was shutting down, while I felt overwhelmed by immediate conversations. We had to learn that not every emotional moment required deep discussion right away. Instead of pushing for instant resolution, we allowed space for emotions to settle, ensuring that conversations happened when both of us were ready rather than in the heat of frustration.

Another challenge we faced was financial decision-making. Research highlights that money is one of the top sources of conflict in marriages (Smith et al., 2022), and this was no exception for us. I approached finances with caution, always planning ahead, while Kathleen tended to focus on flexibility in spending. This difference led to frustration—I wanted a budget that ensured financial security, while she wanted to enjoy small purchases without feeling restricted. We had to have honest conversations about how financial decisions impacted both of us. Instead of arguing about every individual expense, we developed a system that worked for both of us: planning major purchases together, ensuring transparency, and allowing each of us space to make financial decisions independently within a reasonable limit. This eliminated unnecessary stress and helped us work as a team instead of adversaries.

I am highly structured with budgeting, while Kathleen prefers flexibility. At first, we avoided deep discussions about money because we didn't want to argue. However, ignoring financial concerns only caused frustration to build. Instead of avoiding the topic, we created scheduled discussions where we calmly reviewed our expenses and savings, ensuring that money wouldn't become a lingering issue between us. Kathleen usually prints our income and expense so I can review and I have idea of what we have financially.

One difficult lesson in choosing battles wisely is letting go of past conflicts. Many couples struggle because they bring up old disagreements during new arguments, making resolution harder. There will be moments when frustrations will resurface in unrelated conversations, causing tension that isn't necessary. Studies emphasize that couples who forgive and move forward after conflicts experience greater emotional resilience (Williams & Thompson, 2021). Holding onto past issues only deepened resentment, making future disagreements more emotionally charged. We made the conscious choice to close the door on unresolved conflicts and focus on building solutions rather than revisiting old wounds.

Parenting brought another layer of conflict resolution into our relationship. As parents, we had different approaches in handling challenges with our seven children. I favoured structured discipline, ensuring consistency, while Kathleen leaned more toward flexibility. At times, we clashed on decisions about how to set rules and enforce expectations. Instead of seeing our differences as opposing forces, we had to recognize the value in both approaches—structure provided stability, while flexibility allowed space for individuality. Once we understood that parenting styles weren't about one being right and the other being wrong, but rather about finding balance, we developed a parenting system that incorporated elements of both.

Disagreements over emotional expression were another area where we had to be mindful of choosing our battles. I am naturally expressive, feeling emotions deeply and openly, while Kathleen tends to process internally before speaking. This difference led to misunderstandings—I felt like she was distant, while she felt like conversations were happening before she was ready to engage. Studies suggest that people process emotions differently and forcing immediate resolution can lead to frustration instead of clarity (Smith et al., 2022). We had to learn that not every emotional moment needed an immediate conversation. Instead, we created space for reflection, ensuring that discussions happened when both of us were ready rather than during heightened emotions.

Choosing battles wisely is understanding when to let go. Couples often find themselves arguing over insignificant details—what movie to watch, which restaurant to eat at, or whose turn it is to do a small household task. Minor frustrations can turn into unnecessary disagreements simply because we let emotions dictate our conversation. Studies highlight that letting small frustrations go rather than escalating them into full arguments significantly improves marital satisfaction (Johnson & Green, 2020). Instead of dwelling on minor differences, we shifted our focus to making decisions based on kindness rather than frustration.

Through experience, we have discovered that choosing battles wisely does not mean avoiding conflict—it means engaging in discussions that truly matter while letting go of arguments that add no value to the relationship. Research suggests that couples who prioritize emotional connection over proving a point tend to have stronger, more resilient relationships (Williams & Thompson, 2021). We must embrace this principle in our daily interactions, ensuring that our approach challenges our perspective, patience, and mutual respect.

At the core of choosing battles wisely is the realization that love is more important than the need to be right. When couples learn to evaluate the significance of an argument before engaging in it, they can maintain peace, reduce stress, and strengthen their emotional bond. We should learn when to discuss, when to let go, and when to compromise to make our marriage stronger. Instead of allowing conflict to pull us apart, we should use it as a tool for growth, understanding, and deeper emotional connection.

Choosing Battles Wisely

One lessons to learn in your marriage is that not every disagreement deserves to turn into a full-blown argument. Early on in our marriage, we've found ourselves engaging in frustrating discussions over things that, in hindsight, didn't hold enough significance to justify the emotional drain they caused. Learning to choose our battles wisely helped us preserve peace, focus on real issues, and keep small frustrations from escalating into unnecessary tension.

One realization we had was that some arguments were less about resolving a real issue and more about proving a point. Whether it was how the laundry should be folded, which direction the pillows on the couch should face, or whether the dishes needed to be washed immediately after dinner, we found ourselves caught up in small conflicts that didn't truly affect our relationship. Instead of giving energy to these discussions, we learned to ask: *Does this disagreement affect our happiness, emotional connection, or core values?* If the answer was no, then it was better to let it go rather than let frustration linger.

Kathleen likes the house to be cool, while I prefer a slightly warmer temperature. At one point, we found ourselves constantly adjusting the thermostat, each trying to create the "perfect" climate without realizing it was turning into an actual problem. Instead of arguing every time one of us made a change, we sat down and compromised—agreeing to keep the thermostat at a middle setting and using blankets or fans to adjust individually as needed. The issue itself wasn't worth disrupting our daily peace, and this simple adjustment eliminated unnecessary tension.

Every disagreement carries an emotional toll. learn to ask: *Will this argument bring us closer together, or will it create unnecessary distance?* If the issue wasn't something that genuinely affected your marriage in a deep way, the cost of arguing often isn't worth the emotional energy it drains.

For a while, I was frustrated when Kathleen left lights on in the rooms, she wasn't in. I brought it up multiple times, assuming it was about saving energy or maintaining order. But after a discussion, I realized she simply preferred bright spaces and didn't think twice about switching them off when moving from one room to another. Instead of allowing this minor habit to create unnecessary conflict, we agreed that if it truly bothered me, I could turn them off without making it a recurring issue between us.

One mistake most couples make is treating personality differences as problems rather than accepting them as part of their partner's individuality. Some of your disagreements aren't about issues that needed resolving—they were just differences in how you approach daily life. Recognizing this will allow you to

Choosing Battles Wisely

stop trying to "fix" each other and instead embrace those differences with patience.

I like structured plans, while I Kathleen tend to be more flexible. In the beginning, this caused conflict—I wanted plans made in advance, while she preferred to keep options open. Instead of arguing over which approach was "correct," we realized that neither way was wrong—it was just a personality difference. We learned to blend our styles by scheduling important plans while leaving room for spontaneous moments, ensuring that both of us felt comfortable.

While some conflicts aren't worth engaging in, there are moments when avoiding discussions can create resentment. Certain issues—such as emotional needs, parenting decisions, and financial concerns—are worth addressing in a constructive way.

Not every disagreement needs a serious resolution—sometimes, laughter is the best way to move past small frustrations. Humor lightens the emotional weight of minor issues; it helps shift your focus to what really matters.

For weeks, I kept noticing that kitchen cabinet doors were left open randomly throughout the day, but neither of us admitted to forgetting to close it. Instead of turning it into a disagreement, we turned it into a joke—each pretending the other was a "suspect" in a mysterious case. What could have been a moment of blame became a shared joke instead of an argument, reminding us that not everything needs to be taken seriously.

Choosing battles wisely is one of the most valuable skills in marriage. Not every disagreement needs to be "won"—sometimes, it's better to preserve peace than to insist on proving a point. By understanding which issues require discussion and which ones can be let go, couples can protect emotional connection, reduce unnecessary stress, and ensure that disagreements serve a purpose rather than becoming a recurring source of frustration.

Choosing battles wisely in marriage is about protecting peace, prioritizing important discussions, and letting go of unnecessary conflicts. You will learn that through experience not every issue deserves emotional energy and focusing on meaningful conversations helps prevent tension from draining the relationship. Here are some practical tips we've applied that can help couples navigate disagreements effectively.

TIPS TO REMEMBER:

1. Ask Yourself: Is This Worth the Emotional Toll?

Before engaging in an argument, pause and ask: *Will this issue still matter in a week, a month, or a year?*

- If the answer is no, it may be best to let it go.
- If the issue affects emotional connection, trust, or long-term happiness, it's worth addressing.

Small frustrations—like how towels should be folded—aren't worth disrupting the peace, but bigger concerns—like finances or emotional connection—require real conversations.

2. Recognize When Exhaustion or Stress Is Driving Conflict

Many arguments happen not because of real issues, but because of stress, fatigue, or frustration from external pressures.

- Before reacting, ask: *Am I upset because of this issue, or is something else influencing my emotions?*
- If exhaustion is amplifying the frustration, wait until both partners are calm before engaging in discussion.

Learn to avoid as many unnecessary conflicts as possible by simply recognizing when stress makes small concerns feel larger than they actually are.

3. Don't Turn Every Personality Difference Into a Problem

Couples sometimes clash not because of real issues, but because they expect their partner to think or behave exactly like them.

- Instead of debating over different habits or perspectives, recognize that differences aren't problems—they're natural parts of individuality.
- Work on blending approaches rather than forcing one way over the other.

Kathleen enjoys planning things ahead, while I prefer a more flexible approach. Instead of arguing about which method is "right," we've learned to combine structure with spontaneity, ensuring both of us feel comfortable.

4. Let Go of the Need to Be Right

Winning an argument doesn't necessarily strengthen a relationship—it often creates emotional distance.

- Shift the focus from who is right to how you can solve the problem together.
- If being "right" causes unnecessary emotional harm, it may be better to step back and prioritize peace instead.

Proving a point isn't as valuable as protecting emotional connection, and many disagreements are resolved more effectively through understanding rather than proving a stance.

5. Focus on Solutions, Not Frustration

Arguments often escalate because couples spend more time repeating their frustration rather than working toward a resolution.

- Instead of saying, *"You always do this,"* shift to, *"How can we prevent this from happening again?"*
- Approach discussions with problem-solving energy rather than blame or defensiveness.

We've applied this every time in a disagreement—rather than cycling through frustration, we move toward finding solutions, ensuring that conflict leads to growth rather than resentment.

6. Use Humor to Diffuse Small Conflicts

Some frustrations don't need serious conversations—they need laughter and lightheartedness.

- If an issue isn't major, inject humour into the moment instead of turning it into a source of tension.
- Find ways to turn small annoyances into playful interactions rather than arguments.

We've prevented many unnecessary conflicts simply by laughing about small frustrations rather than making them personal.

7. Protect Emotional Intimacy Over Proving a Point

Every discussion should lead toward deeper understanding, not emotional harm.

- If a conversation begins to drain trust or connection, step back and reassess whether the issue is worth engaging in.
- A healthy marriage isn't built on who is right—it's built on mutual respect and emotional security.

When we prioritize emotional connection over frustration, disagreements become opportunities for growth instead of division.

Effective Communication

Speaking with Love and Clarity

Communication is the foundation of conflict resolution. Without it, misunderstandings can escalate into frustration and resentment. We've learned that the way we speak to each other during a disagreement matters just as much as the message we want to convey.

Communication is the foundation of every successful relationship. Without it, misunderstandings can fester, emotions can be misinterpreted, and small concerns can escalate into deeper frustrations. Effective communication is not just about talking—it's about speaking with love, listening with intention, and ensuring that our words build rather than break down the connection between us. The way we express ourselves during disagreements or emotionally charged moments can strengthen trust or weaken it, depending on how we approach our conversations.

We've learned that love should guide the way we communicate, even in conflict. Studies highlight that couples who prioritize respectful dialogue rather than reactive responses experience greater long-term relationship satisfaction (Smith et al., 2022). We've had moments when frustration led to sharp words, assumptions, and unnecessary emotional wounds. It wasn't that we didn't love each other—it was that stress, exhaustion, or personal insecurities sometimes influenced how we spoke. When we realized that words carry weight, we became more intentional about choosing language that reflects care rather than criticism.

A major challenge in communication is assuming rather than asking. Many couples believe they understand their partner's thoughts and emotions without needing clarification, but research suggests that unchecked assumptions often lead to misinterpretation (Johnson & Green, 2020). We've had moments when we thought we knew what the other was feeling, only to later realize we had misunderstood the situation entirely. For example, I used to assume that when Kathleen was quiet, she was upset. In reality, she was simply processing her thoughts. This misunderstanding led to unnecessary conversations where I would press for explanations when she wasn't ready to express them, creating tension. Over time, we learned the importance of asking rather than assuming—checking in with each other rather than jumping to conclusions.

Tone and delivery matter just as much as the words themselves. Many couples don't realize that how something is said can impact how the message is received (Williams & Thompson, 2021). We've learned that frustration in our tone could make neutral statements feel confrontational. If I said something in a hurried or irritated manner, even if the words weren't offensive, Kathleen felt the emotional tension behind them. Likewise, when Kathleen expressed concerns with an overwhelmed tone, I felt criticized even if her words weren't directly negative. Studies show that communicating with a softened tone during disagreements leads to higher emotional understanding and resolution (Smith et al., 2022). Once we became mindful of not just what we said, but how we said it, our conversations became healthier and more productive.

Listening is just as important as speaking, yet many couples struggle with truly hearing each other's concerns. Active listening—where one partner fully absorbs what the other is saying before responding—reduces defensiveness and enhances emotional connection (Johnson & Green, 2020). We've had moments when we were so focused on preparing a response that we didn't fully take in what the other person was saying. This led to misinterpretation and unresolved frustrations. We learned that genuine listening means pausing, processing, and responding with care rather than reacting immediately.

One effective strategy we implemented was using "I" statements rather than "You" accusations. Research highlights that phrase like "You never listen" or "You always do this" put people on the defensive, making resolution more difficult (Williams & Thompson, 2021). Instead, shifting to statements such as *"I feel unheard when..."* or *"I feel frustrated when this happens"* changes the conversation from blame to problem-solving. We've noticed a dramatic improvement in how we understood each other once we focused on expressing our emotions rather than pointing fingers.

Another challenge in communication is timing and environment. Not all conversations should happen immediately, especially when emotions are heightened. Studies show that delaying conflict discussions until emotions settle leads to more constructive conversations (Smith et al., 2022). We've realized that we had to choose the right moments to engage in serious discussions. If we were tired, overwhelmed, or distracted, trying to resolve conflicts only led to further frustration. Instead, we started setting aside intentional time for discussions, ensuring that our conversations happened when both of us could engage with patience and clarity.

Expressing appreciation through words also plays a vital role in effective communication. While conflict resolution is an important skill, maintaining a strong emotional connection through daily encouragement, validation, and kindness helps prevent many arguments before they start. Research highlights that couples who regularly express gratitude and appreciation toward each other experience higher relationship satisfaction (Johnson & Green, 2020). We've found that even small affirmations—whether it's acknowledging effort, expressing admiration, or simply saying "thank you" for something simple—strengthen emotional security. The more positive interactions we build into our daily conversations, the more resilient we become in moments of conflict.

Through all these experiences, we've learned that effective communication is not just about talking—it's about ensuring that every conversation strengthens our connection rather than weakens it. By embracing clarity, patience, kindness, and intentional listening, couples can build stronger, more fulfilling relationships that withstand challenges. When communication is guided by love, understanding replaces frustration, and unity becomes the foundation for every discussion.

Effective communication in marriage is about more than just talking—it's about ensuring that conversations build connection rather than create distance. The way we speak, listen, and interpret each other's emotions directly influences the health of our relationship. Communication shapes how couples resolve conflict, express love, share burdens, and support each other through life's challenges. Without it, misunderstandings flourish, assumptions replace clarity, and emotions get lost in translation.

One lessons we've learned is that communication is an ongoing process, not just a skill applied in moments of conflict. Many couples believe that good communication is only needed when solving problems, but in reality, everyday conversations are just as important. Studies show that consistent, positive interaction fosters deeper emotional security, preventing the build-up of tension (Smith et al., 2022). We've made it a habit to check in with each other—not just about major decisions, but about the small things too. Whether it's sharing thoughts about our day, discussing goals, or simply laughing together over something trivial, these moments reinforce trust and emotional connection.

We've also learned that effective communication includes nonverbal cues, such as tone, facial expressions, and body language. Research highlights that over 70% of communication is nonverbal, meaning that gestures, posture, and facial expressions often speak louder than words (Johnson & Green, 2020). When frustration builds up, even when words are polite, our body language sometimes communicated a different message. A tense posture, crossed arms, or even the absence of eye contact could signal withdrawal, making meaningful dialogue harder. Becoming more aware of these nonverbal elements allowed us to adjust our approach—ensuring that our tone and presence matched our intention.

Another crucial element of communication is understanding differences in processing emotions. We all experience conflict differently, which affected how we communicated during disagreements. Some individuals tend to think through their emotions internally before verbalizing them, while others prefer to express their feelings right away and process them as they speak. I like immediate discussion while Kathleen needs time to reflect before talking. Studies indicate that forcing immediate conversations can lead to frustration, while allowing space for emotions to settle fosters healthier communication (Williams & Thompson, 2021). Once we acknowledge these differences, we can adjust our approach. Instead of pressuring each other to engage in discussions before feeling ready, we can find a balance—giving ourselves room to express emotions while allowing our spouse time to process before responding.

One powerful technique we incorporated into our communication is reflective listening—repeating and summarizing what the other person says before responding. Research suggests that couples who practice reflective listening have stronger emotional bonds and fewer misunderstandings (Smith et al., 2022). For example, instead of immediately reacting when Kathleen shares a concern, I'll say, *"I hear that you're feeling overwhelmed because of how busy this week has been. You need more support with the schedule, is that right?"* This ensures that I truly understand her perspective before offering a response. Likewise, when I express my feelings, she listens carefully before responding with reassurance or problem-solving. Reflective listening removes assumptions, ensures clarity, and reinforces the feeling of being heard.

We've embraced learning to speak with kindness, even in disagreement. Many couples struggle with harsh words during arguments, believing that frustration justifies criticism. However, studies show that negative communication patterns—such as blame, sarcasm, or dismissiveness—lead to long-term resentment, even after the conflict is resolved (Johnson & Green, 2020).

We've made a commitment to choose words that strengthen rather than harm, even when discussing difficult topics. Instead of saying, *"You never listen to me,"* I shift to, *"I feel unheard when this happens."* This small change keeps the conversation solution-focused rather than confrontational. Likewise, Kathleen replaced statements like, *"You don't care,"* with *"I need to feel more supported in this."* These language adjustments diffuse tension, making discussions more productive rather than emotionally charged.

Validation is another crucial aspect of communication that often gets overlooked. People want to feel that their emotions, perspectives, and concerns are valued, even if their partner doesn't fully agree with them. Research suggests that validating your partner's feelings—acknowledging their emotions without judgment—creates a stronger emotional connection (Williams & Thompson, 2021).

We've learned that responding with phrases like *"I see why that upset you"* or *"I understand why that situation was frustrating"* reinforces emotional security. Validation is not about agreeing with everything—it's about acknowledging the importance of your partner's feelings.

As part of our commitment to effective communication, we also introduced intentional conversation time, which is where our "30-Minute Thursdays" practice comes in. This dedicated time allows us to focus entirely on meaningful discussion without distractions, ensuring that important conversations receive thoughtful attention rather than rushed reactions. Studies suggest that setting aside intentional time for communication improves emotional intimacy and conflict resolution (Smith et al., 2022). By committing to consistent, distraction-free discussions, couples reinforce connection and prevent misunderstandings from building up over time.

Through experience, we have learned that communication in marriage is not about talking more—it's about talking effectively. By incorporating clear dialogue, active listening, emotional awareness, and kindness, couples can build deeper trust, minimize conflict, and strengthen their emotional bond. The goal is not just to communicate—but to ensure that every conversation brings clarity, connection, and deeper understanding.

Effective communication is one of the most powerful tools in marriage, allowing couples to deepen understanding, resolve conflicts productively, and strengthen emotional intimacy. We've found that the way we communicate in both everyday conversations and moments of disagreement directly impacts our connection. Over time, we've adopted strategies that help reduce misunderstandings, foster patience, and ensure that every discussion strengthens rather than weakens our relationship.

TIPS TO REMEMBER:

1. Listening Before Responding

One of the biggest mistakes couples make in communication is responding before fully understanding the other person's point of view. Pausing to listen instead of reacting immediately significantly will improve your discussions. Instead of assuming what the other person means, take time to hear the full thought, process it, and then respond thoughtfully. This prevents knee-jerk reactions, which can sometimes escalate tension unnecessarily.

Tip: Practice active listening by maintaining eye contact, nodding to show engagement, and repeating key points to confirm understanding before offering a response.

2. Using "I" Statements Instead of Accusations

When frustration builds, it's easy to slip into accusatory language, which often leads to defensiveness. We discovered that shifting the focus from blame to personal experience creates a more productive conversation. Saying *"I feel hurt when..."* instead of *"You never listen"* keeps the discussion solution-oriented rather than emotionally charged.

Example from our marriage: There were times when Kathleen felt overwhelmed by household responsibilities but felt hesitant to bring it up. Instead of saying, *"You don't help enough around the house,"* she shifted her approach to *"I feel exhausted when I carry most of the responsibilities alone. I need more support."* This small change allowed me to understand her feelings rather than feel criticized, which led to a constructive solution instead of an argument.

Tip: Whenever addressing concerns, start with how you feel rather than pointing fingers. This approach fosters openness and reduces defensiveness.

Effective Communication

3. Avoiding Emotional Bullying

Words can either heal or wound, and we have learned to choose them wisely, especially in moments of frustration. Emotional bullying—raising voices, sarcasm, or belittling remarks—only weakens trust. When discussions became too emotionally charged, neither person will feel heard, and the conversation will lose its purpose. Instead, committed to speaking with patience, even in disagreements, ensuring that frustration doesn't turn into emotional harm.

Tip: If emotions are overwhelming a discussion, take a short break before continuing. Revisiting the issue after calming down often leads to better solutions rather than impulsive reactions.

4. Creating a Safe Space for Open Communication

A major factor in effective communication is feeling safe to express emotions, concerns, and needs without fear of judgment. Avoid shutting down discussions or dismissing each other's feelings, even if you don't fully agree. This helped foster an environment where you could talk openly without fear of criticism.

Tip: Encourage discussions where both partners can express themselves honestly without interruptions or invalidation. Make it a habit to check in with each other about thoughts, feelings, and concerns.

5. Understanding Timing in Conversations

Not all discussions should happen immediately, especially when emotions are heightened. We learned that pushing to resolve an issue before both of us are ready can make conversations counterproductive. Instead, choosing the right moment to talk ensures the conversation is more rational and effective.

Example from our marriage: There were times when I wanted to solve a disagreement right away, but Kathleen needed time to process before talking. Rather than forcing the conversation before she was ready, I learned to give her space, ensuring that when we did talk, it was more productive.

Tip: If one or both partners need time before discussing an issue, communicate that need. Saying *"I want to talk about this, but I need time to process first"* allows for a healthy approach to conflict resolution.

6. Practicing Daily Check-Ins

Communication isn't just for problem-solving—it's also about strengthening connection through everyday conversation. Introduce daily check-ins where you can take time to ask each other about your day, how you're feeling, and anything weighing on your hearts. This simple practice helps stay emotionally aligned, ensuring that you're in tune with each other's thoughts and feelings.

Tip: Spend at least 10-15 minutes each day checking in with your partner. This prevents emotional distance and fosters deeper understanding.

7. Expressing Appreciation and Encouragement

Many couples focus on what needs improvement but recognizing what's already working well strengthens emotional security. Make it a habit to express appreciation in daily conversations, ensuring that neither of you feels taken for granted. Even small affirmations—like acknowledging each other's efforts—make a big difference.

Tip: Make a habit of saying thank you, I appreciate you, or I love you in daily interactions. Encouragement builds trust and emotional closeness.

Effective communication isn't about never disagreeing—it's about navigating conversations with clarity, patience, and respect. We've learned that the way we speak to each other, the words we choose, and the emotional atmosphere of our discussions directly affect the strength of our marriage. By listening with intention, using gentle language, avoiding emotional harm, and prioritizing connection, couples can transform communication into a tool for deepening love rather than creating distance.

SEPARATING THE PROBLEM

Problems Are Not Enemies

One of the biggest mistakes couples make in conflict is viewing each other as the problem rather than working together to solve the issue. You are on the same team, even when you don't see things eye to eye.

Instead of thinking, *"Kathleen is frustrating me"*, I now frame my thoughts as, *"This issue is frustrating me, and I need to find a way to address it with Kathleen in a healthy way."*

We've learned in marriage the importance of separating the problem from the person. In the early

Separating The Problem

years, when conflict arose, it was easy to fall into the trap of seeing each other as the cause of frustration, rather than recognizing the actual issue that was creating the tension. This pattern led to defensiveness, hurt feelings, and unresolved emotions because instead of working as a team, we were reacting as individuals caught in disagreement. Over time, we realized that the true challenge wasn't Kathleen or me—it was the problem itself.

Problems in marriage can be like leeches, slowly draining love, peace, and understanding if they aren't properly identified and removed. A disagreement about finances isn't necessarily about money—it may be about security, trust, or feeling valued in decision-making. Conflict over household responsibilities isn't always about chores—it might stem from feeling underappreciated or overwhelmed. We've discovered that if we focus on an issue that exists rather than blaming each other, we could resolve challenges more effectively and strengthen our relationship rather than weaken it.

Problems in marriage don't arrive randomly—they always have a cause, whether it's external stress, personal insecurities, differences in upbringing, or simply exhaustion from daily life. We've learned that once we acknowledged the source, we are able to neutralize conflict before it became personal. Two people working together toward a solution will always be stronger than one person struggling alone.

The turning point in our relationship was when we stopped seeing each other as the issue and started treating the problem as the real enemy. Instead of battling each other, we began battling whatever was trying to steal joy, peace, and unity from our marriage. The moment that shift happened, our relationship became more resilient, our conversations more productive, and our love more secure.

By separating the problem from the person, we have found that conflict no longer drains our marriage—it strengthens it, giving us the ability to move forward with wisdom, patience, and an unshakable commitment to each other.

One important realization we've had in our marriage is that problems are not the enemy—how we handle them is. Every couple faces challenges, whether minor daily frustrations or deeper, long-term struggles. Many couples unknowingly start seeing each other as the problem, rather than identifying the actual issue causing tension. Over time, we learned that separating the problem from the person was the key to working together rather than against each other.

Through these experiences, we've learned that the real enemy in marriage is not each other—it's the problems that, if unchecked, create division. By identifying issues objectively rather than emotionally, couples can replace frustration with understanding and resentment with teamwork. Once we stopped fighting each other and started fighting the actual problems, our relationship became more peaceful, resilient, and deeply connected. Every couple has the ability to turn challenges into opportunities for growth—the key is knowing that two people solving a problem together will always be stronger than one person handling it alone.

TIPS TO REMEMBER:

1. Identify the Root Cause

Before reacting, take a step back and ask: *What is the real issue here?*

- Is it stress, miscommunication, unmet expectations, or past experiences influencing the moment?
- Instead of assuming your spouse is the problem, examine the situation objectively.

There are moments when frustration can feel personal, but once you pinpointed the actual source of tension, realized the issue wasn't each other—the external stress affects how you communicated.

2. Pause Before Responding

It's easy to react emotionally, especially in moments of disagreement. Instead of jumping to conclusions, try:

- Taking a deep breath before responding.
- Reframing thoughts from *"You're frustrating me"* to *"This situation is frustrating, how can we fix it together?"*

Pausing before engaging in heated discussions prevents unnecessary emotional damage and allowed for more effective problem-solving.

3. Talk Like a Team, Not Opponents

Shifting language from blame to collaboration makes a huge difference. Instead of saying:

- *"You never listen to me,"* try *"I feel unheard when this happens."*
- *"Why do you always do this?"* try *"Let's figure out a way to handle this better."*

Changing your words helps shift your perspective—turning conflict into constructive conversations instead of battles.

4. Make Problem-Solving a Priority

After identifying the issue, work together to find solutions rather than proving who's right.

- Ask "How can we prevent this from happening again?"

- Consider compromise, shared responsibilities, and alternative approaches.

In marriage, two people problem-solving together will always be stronger than one person handling frustration alone. Actively working toward solutions instead of reliving frustration can create growth rather than resentment.

5. Remove Emotional "Leeches" From Your Relationship

Some problems linger, subtly draining trust and connection. Ask yourself:

- Are past hurts creeping into new conversations?
- Are external influences adding unnecessary pressure?
- Is an unresolved issue causing repeated tension?

Holding onto old conflicts will make new discussions harder. Instead, make a habit of fully resolving issues, letting go, and moving forward rather than dragging past problems into future conversations.

6. Strengthen Your Partnership Through Respect

Conflict doesn't mean failure—it's an opportunity for growth, deeper understanding, and stronger teamwork. Couples who respect each other even during disagreements create a foundation that lasts.

- Express appreciation even after a disagreement.
- Recognize each other's efforts in working toward resolution.
- Remind yourselves that you're in this together, not against each other.

The more respect and patience you show each other, the easier it is to navigate challenges without resentment.

Separating the problem from the person requires intentional effort, but when couples choose teamwork over opposition, they replace frustration with unity, strengthening their marriage instead of allowing difficulties to weaken it.

Separating The Problem

talented, couples who respect each other over damning disagreements create a bump on the mast.

- Represent one method even after a disagreement.
- Recognize each other's effort in working toward a solution.
- Remind yourselves that you're in this together, not against each other.

The more respect and patience you show each other, the easier it is to navigate challenges without resentment.

Separating the problem from the person requires intentional effort, but when couples choose teamwork over opposition, they replace frustration with unity. Subsequently, their marriage instead of allowing difficulties to weaken it.

COMMON GROUND

COMPROMISE

Compromise is not about losing or giving in, but about working together toward solutions that benefit both partners. Your will face moments when your perspectives are completely different—whether in parenting, finances, or handling daily responsibilities. In those moments, rather than trying to "win" the disagreement, find middle ground, ensuring that both of your feelings and needs are respected.

Finding common ground in marriage is essential—not just for maintaining peace, but for honouring the partnership God has called us to. As Christians, we must remember that marriage is not just about two individuals—it is about becoming one in spirit, mind, and purpose. This means learning how to work together, resolve differences with love, and move forward in unity, especially when compromise is needed.

One of the biggest misconceptions about compromise is that one person must "give in" while the other wins. But compromise in a Christ-centered marriage is not about winning or losing—it's about finding solutions that strengthen both partners. We've faced moments when our perspectives seemed opposite, but instead of fighting to prove our point, we asked: *How can we work together to honor each other and God through this decision?*

In Philippians 2:2-4, Paul reminds us to be like-minded, having the same love, being of one spirit and purpose, and to value others above ourselves. This applies to marriage—rather than insisting on our way, we choose to prioritize the relationship over personal preference.

In Genesis 2:24, the Bible tells us that *a man shall leave his father and mother and be joined to his wife, and they shall become one flesh.* That means marriage is not about two people going separate ways—it's about walking the same path together. But unity does not mean identical thinking; it means learning to embrace each other's strengths while navigating differences with wisdom.

We've discovered this truth when we faced disagreements in parenting, finances, and life decisions. Instead of viewing our differences as roadblocks, we saw them as opportunities to grow in understanding and deepen our relationship. When we moved beyond personal preferences and focused on the unity God desires, we found greater peace in our marriage.

A Christ-centered marriage thrives when both individuals commit to unity rather than separation. In Colossians 3:14, we are reminded that *love binds everything together in perfect harmony*. Embrace this truth—instead of letting disagreements create distance, use them to draw closer, seeking God's guidance in every decision.

By choosing to love over frustration, compromise over stubbornness, and unity over division, couples create a marriage that is built on faith, strengthened by understanding, and rooted in the partnership that God intended.

Finding common ground in marriage is one of the most powerful ways to foster unity, resolve conflict, and strengthen emotional connection. It requires intentional effort, humility, and a willingness to see situations from both perspectives rather than simply defending one's own. Without common ground, disagreements linger, division grows, and emotional distance forms. But when you commit to understanding each other, valuing compromise, and working as a team, you strengthen the foundation of your relationship and create a marriage filled with peace and mutual respect.

One obstacle to finding common ground is pride and it stubbornness. It's natural to want things to go our way or believe our perspective is the most logical. But marriage is not about proving points—it's about working together to reach solutions that honor both people involved. There were times when we've let pride get in the way of healthy resolution. Whether it was deciding how to spend our weekends, parenting choices, or financial decisions, we had moments when we both felt strongly about our viewpoint. It was only when we let go of the need to "win" and instead focused on understanding each other's perspective that we truly moved forward.

When frustration rises, it's easy to become reactive rather than constructive, causing conversations to escalate rather than resolve. We've noticed this happens during discussions about daily routines—things like household responsibilities, schedules, and personal habits. Instead of treating these discussions as opportunities for teamwork, we sometimes let emotions dictate the conversation.

One essential part of finding common ground is respecting individual strengths and weaknesses. No two people will ever be exactly alike, which means compromise involves leveraging strengths to balance weaknesses instead of forcing change. In our early years of marriage, this difference caused tension, but rather than trying to make one of us conform to the other's way of thinking, we used both strengths to enhance our relationship. Kathleen's organization helped with long-term planning, while my flexibility allowed us to navigate unexpected changes without stress.

A biblical perspective reminds us that marriage is about partnership, not opposition. Ecclesiastes 4:9 states, *"Two are better than one, because they have a good return for their labor."* This means that marriage thrives when both partners contribute, support, and uplift each other rather than competing for control. We've embrace this truth when making decisions—we recognize that God has called us to walk together, not separately, and in every challenge, we ask ourselves: *What choice strengthens us as a couple rather than dividing us?*

One major aspect of compromise is learning how to meet in the middle without feeling like one person is sacrificing too much. Many couples fear that compromises means giving up their needs to accommodate their spouse, but this is not true. We've learned that compromise is not about loss—it's about adjusting in a way that respects both people. For example, in situations where we had different desires—such as choosing vacation destinations—we blended our preferences rather than having only one person decide.

Common Ground

Instead of feeling like one of us was missing out, we created experiences that honored both of our wishes, strengthening unity rather than creating resentment.

Forgiveness plays a key role in finding common ground. Past conflicts, if not fully resolved, can block couples from moving forward, making it difficult to establish compromise. Kathleen and I had moments when previous frustrations resurfaced in new discussions, making resolution harder than it needed to be. We realized that without closing the door on past wounds, we couldn't truly reach agreement on new topics. We committed to fully resolving past issues before moving on, ensuring that old resentment wouldn't interfere with future discussions.

Ultimately, finding common ground is a commitment to unity, love, and teamwork. It requires letting go of ego, embracing patience, and focusing on the greater goal—the health and happiness of the relationship. We've continued to apply these lessons, knowing that every challenge presents an opportunity to come together rather than pull apart. When couples prioritize understanding, seek God's guidance, and work toward solutions with love rather than frustration, they create a marriage that thrives and withstands every obstacle.

Finding common ground in marriage requires intentional effort and a commitment to unity. Here are some practical tips we've applied to help us compromise effectively while strengthening our bond.

TIPS TO REMEMBER:

1. Prioritize Unity Over Winning

Compromise is not about who is right; it's about what solution works best for both partners. A marriage thrives when both individuals focus on teamwork instead of competition.

Tip: Shift your perspective from *"How do I get my way?"* to *"How can we create a solution that benefits us both?"*

2. Recognize Your Differences Without Trying to Change Each Other

It's easy to fall into the habit of wanting your partner to think and act exactly like you. But marriage is about celebrating individuality while working toward unity.

Tip: Instead of trying to convince your spouse to adopt your approach, ask: *"How can we blend our strengths to create a balanced solution?"*

3. Identify Non-Negotiables and Flexible Areas

Not all issues require full compromise—some involve core values, while others are simply preferences. Certain beliefs should remain intact, while everyday decisions can allow flexibility.

Tip: Determine what truly matters and where adjustments can be made. If an issue affects faith, integrity, or emotional well-being, it requires serious discussion, but if it's about preferences or habits, consider letting go or finding a middle ground.

4. Keep Communication Open and Respectful

Compromise is only possible when both partners feel heard and respected. We've been committed to ensuring that even during disagreements, our tone and words reflect patience, not frustration.

Tip: Express thoughts in a way that builds connection rather than creates division. Saying *"I feel concerned about this"* keeps the discussion open, while *"You always do this"* can lead to defensiveness.

5. Seek God's Guidance in Difficult Decisions

For Christian couples, compromise isn't just about adjusting to each other—it's about seeking God's wisdom in important decisions. We've have learned that when an issue feels difficult to resolve, turning to prayer helps provide clarity.

Tip: Take time to pray together when facing challenging situations. Ask God for guidance, patience, and a solution that strengthens your marriage rather than divides it.

6. Reaffirm Your Commitment After Every Compromise

Compromise requires effort, but it should never feel like defeat. We've make it a habit to express appreciation for each other's willingness to find common ground so that neither of us feels overlooked or undervalued.

Tip: After resolving a disagreement, take a moment to reaffirm love and gratitude, ensuring that compromise leads to unity rather than lingering resentment.

By applying these strategies, couples can navigate differences with patience, strengthen their relationship through healthy compromise, and move forward in unity as God intended.

LOVE OVER CONFLICT

Avoid Damaging Emotional Security

At the heart of conflict resolution is the decision to let love rule instead of allowing arguments to dictate the relationship's emotional climate. We have had tense moments, disagreements, and frustrations, but through it all, we have learned that our love, trust, and commitment must always be stronger than any conflict.

A couple do not let their differences weaken their marriage—they work together, finding solutions, growing, and strengthening their leadership. In the same way, marriage thrives when love leads the way, guiding conversations, decisions, and resolutions with patience, wisdom, and unity.

Love Over Conflict

Love is the foundation of a strong and lasting marriage, and when couples allow unity to take priority over conflict, they create a relationship that withstands challenges rather than being consumed by them. We've learned that disagreements will inevitably arise, but how we approach them determines whether they strengthen or weaken our bond. No matter how serious an issue may seem, we remind ourselves that love should always rule over conflict—not by ignoring problems, but by handling them in a way that prioritizes understanding and connection.

One of the greatest dangers in marriage is letting unresolved conflict dominate the relationship. Couples who allow frustration and resentment to linger risk creating emotional walls that make intimacy, trust, and joy harder to maintain. We've found that when we avoid addressing certain issues, those concerns don't disappear—they just silently built tension until they influenced other aspects of our marriage. Over time, we realized that choosing love means actively resolving conflict rather than letting it overshadow the relationship. True unity isn't about avoiding disagreements—it's about addressing them with patience, wisdom, and the intention to grow together.

Letting love rule requires a shift in perspective. Instead of viewing conflict as a battle to prove who is right, couples need to see disagreements as an opportunity to understand each other more deeply.

We've committed to making every discussion serve a purpose rather than simply expressing frustration. When love is at the center of conflict resolution, conversations focus on solutions, respect, and shared goals, rather than lingering on blame or past mistakes.

A key part of letting unity rule is handling disagreements without damaging the emotional security of the marriage. Conflict should never create distance—it should lead to greater closeness by reinforcing communication, mutual respect, and compromise. We practice making sure that even difficult conversations remind us of the strength of our relationship. We do this by reassuring each other that, despite a moment of frustration, our love is more significant than any disagreement. Love-driven conflict resolution allows couples to approach challenges with grace rather than hostility, ensuring that problems are solved without harming the emotional foundation of the marriage.

One practical way to let love rule over conflict is to step away from emotional intensity before engaging in a discussion. When frustration runs high, words can be sharper than intended, and conversations can escalate unnecessarily. We've learned that taking a moment to pause before discussing an issue helps us approach it with a clear mindset rather than reacting impulsively. Addressing conflict from a place of calmness ensures that solutions remain the focus rather than emotions overpowering the discussion.

For Christian couples, scripture reminds us that unity is central to marriage. In Colossians 3:14, we are told, *"And over all these virtues put on love, which binds them all together in perfect unity."* This verse highlights that love is not just a feeling—it is a choice that holds a relationship together, ensuring that conflicts do not dictate the strength of the marriage. We turn to faith as a foundation, allowing God's love to guide how we treat each other, even in moments of disagreement.

Ultimately, letting love rule over conflict means keeping perspective, handling problems with care, and choosing unity over division. We continue to embrace these principles, knowing that every challenge presents an opportunity to deepen understanding, strengthen commitment, and reinforce the love that brought us together. When couples actively choose love-driven conflict resolution, they create a marriage that stands firm, even in difficult moments.

Modern relationships face a unique set of challenges compared to past generations, and couples today must learn to navigate conflict, expectations, and communication in a world that constantly shifts and evolves. We've experienced firsthand how changing societal norms, the influence of technology, and the pressures of daily life impact relationships, and we have had to adjust how we handle conflict to maintain unity and prioritize love in our marriage.

One of the challenges couples today face is the constant distractions that pull attention away from meaningful connection. Between work demands, social media, and other obligations, many couples struggle to dedicate quality time to one another without interference from outside influences. We've noticed earlier on in our relationship that moments together could easily be interrupted by phone notifications, emails, and the pressure to stay connected to the world rather than each other. We realized that conflict often arose not because we didn't love each other, but because we weren't giving our relationship the full presence it deserved.

Another issue modern couples encounter is balancing independence with togetherness. The world encourages individuality and personal growth, which is essential, but sometimes this mindset makes it difficult for couples to prioritize unity over personal ambition. We've found that in certain seasons, we are so focused on our individual goals that we unintentionally neglected our teamwork in marriage. Whether it was career progression, personal hobbies, or social commitments, we had to make a conscious choice to keep our partnership strong while supporting each other's personal dreams.

Technology plays a huge role in modern relationships, and while it offers convenience, it can also create unintentional barriers to communication. We've noticed how easy it is to text instead of talk, scroll through social media instead of engaging in conversation, and rely on digital interaction rather than face-to-face connection. When conflict arose, we had to make sure we weren't using technology as a way to avoid meaningful discussions. Over time, we made it a habit to set aside designated time for conversation without screens, ensuring that when we communicated, it was intentional and focused on strengthening our marriage.

Another challenge couples today face is the overwhelming pressure to compare their relationship to others. Social media often presents an unrealistic version of relationships, showing only the highlight reel rather than the real struggles couples go through. We've fell into the trap of wondering if we were "falling behind" based on the images of perfect vacations, grand gestures, and constantly happy moments we saw online. But we soon realized that love isn't measured by social media posts—it's built in the unseen moments of patience, sacrifice, and honest conversation.

In today's world, couples also deal with changing expectations in household responsibilities and gender roles, blue and pink. We've had different influences growing up, and had to navigate how to divide responsibilities without allowing societal pressures to dictate our roles. Some relationships struggle because one partner assumes certain tasks should fall entirely on the other, leading to imbalance and frustration. We learned that fair division of responsibilities is key to maintaining peace, and instead of following external expectations, we created a system that fit our strengths, personalities, and mutual goals.

Ultimately, couples today must fight for unity amidst distractions, expectations, and external pressures. We've learned that love must always take priority, and while the world constantly changes, the foundation of our marriage remains rooted in patience, trust, and the willingness to grow together rather than apart. The key is not just addressing conflicts when they arise, but creating a relationship where unity is the standard, rather than the exception.

Here are some practical tips for ensuring that love takes priority over conflict, allowing couples to build a strong, united marriage despite challenges:

TIPS TO REMEMBER:

1. Pause Before Engaging in Conflict

When emotions run high, frustration can overshadow clarity, making conversations more reactive than constructive. We've learned that taking a moment to breathe before engaging in difficult conversations helped us communicate more effectively instead of reacting impulsively.

- **Tip:** Before discussing a heated issue, pause for a moment and ask yourself: *Am I responding with love or frustration?*

2. Focus on the Bigger Picture

Many conflicts arise from temporary frustrations, but love lasts beyond disagreements. We remind ourselves that our relationship is bigger than any single argument, so protecting emotional closeness matters more than proving a point.

- **Tip:** Instead of focusing on who is right, ask: *What outcome strengthens our connection rather than causing emotional distance?*

3. Create Safe Spaces for Communication

Couples need an environment where they feel safe expressing their emotions and concerns without fear of criticism or dismissal. We've committed to ensuring that even in disagreements, we speak to each other with respect and patience.

- **Tip:** Make sure discussions are solution-driven rather than centered on blame. Avoid phrases like *"You always do this"* and replace them with *"I feel frustrated when this happens. Can we find a better way?"*

4. Let Small Frustrations Go to Protect Unity

Some disagreements are simply not worth the emotional toll they take on a marriage. Kathleen and I found that choosing to ignore minor frustrations instead of making them constant points of conflict helped maintain peace.

- **Tip:** Ask yourself: *Will this issue matter a month from now?* If not, consider letting it go in favour of unity.

5. Replace Negative Moments with Positive Intentionality

We've noticed that small gestures of kindness helped balance difficult discussions, ensuring that love remained the focus.

- **Tip:** After resolving a conflict, create a positive moment by expressing appreciation, enjoying an activity together, or simply reminding each other why your love is stronger than any disagreement.

6. Pray Together for Strength and Guidance

For Christian couples, love thrives when God is at the center of marriage. Praying together after arguments helped reset our emotions, ensuring that our unity reflected God's love instead of being shaped by frustration.

- **Tip:** When facing ongoing conflict, set time aside to pray for wisdom, patience, and a strengthened bond.

By applying these strategies, couples can approach challenges with intentionality, ensuring that love leads every discussion rather than allowing conflict to overpower connection.

PUTTING CLOSURE TO THE PAST

You Past Does Not Define Your

Old conflicts, if left unresolved, can create resentment in a marriage. One of the most valuable lessons we have learned is to close the chapter on past arguments rather than revisiting them during future disagreements.

When couples carry the weight of unresolved issues, it affects their ability to lead with wisdom and clarity. Letting go of past mistakes allows you to truly heal, preventing small frustrations from turning into larger emotional wounds.

Putting Closure To The Past

One of the barriers to a thriving marriage is the inability to fully put closure to past conflicts. Holding onto old wounds, resentments, and unresolved tensions can quietly erode trust and connection, making it difficult for couples to move forward in unity. Closure is not just about forgetting the past—it's about resolving it in a way that strengthens the future. Without actively choosing to address lingering issues, we risked allowing them to create distance between us.

One of the struggles in marriage is bringing up past mistakes during new arguments. Early in our relationship, we've had moments where frustration from previous disagreements resurfaced, making it difficult to resolve the current issue at hand. Even after discussing and supposedly settling a previous conflict, small remnants of tension would appear again whenever similar situations occurred. This often led to conversations that spiraled away from the original topic, forcing us to relive frustrations that should have already been put to rest. Eventually, we recognized that if we didn't fully close the door on past arguments, they would continue influencing future discussions in unhealthy ways.

Another area where closure was necessary was disappointments in unmet expectations. We all enter into marriage with assumptions—things we believed would naturally happen without needing discussion. Whether it was how we handled household responsibilities, how we expressed affection, or how we divided parenting roles, unspoken expectations sometimes led to silent disappointments. The danger in these situations was allowing resentment to build instead of openly expressing concerns when they first emerged. We learned that addressing frustrations early helped us resolve them instead of letting them linger beneath the surface.

Forgiveness played a major role in putting closure to the past. While disagreements are inevitable, how couples handle them determines whether they deepen their connection or weaken it. We've had moments when pride made it difficult to truly let go, even after apologizing. It wasn't enough to say "I forgive you" if the emotional weight of the issue still lingered in our hearts. True closure required actively choosing to release resentment—not just verbally, but emotionally as well. Holding onto grudges only led to bitterness, which prevented us from experiencing the depth of love that God designed for marriage.

Letting go of past conflicts also meant changing the way we viewed each other's mistakes. We've had moments when one of us fell short—whether in communication, emotional support, or personal responsibilities. Instead of keeping score of who had hurt whom, we learned that grace was far more important than proving a point. When couples allow past mistakes to shape how they see each other, they begin to view their spouse through the lens of past failures rather than present growth. We made a decision to see who we were becoming, rather than simply remembering our weaknesses.

For Christian couples, closure is deeply connected to faith. God calls us to forgive, not because the other person is perfect, but because love cannot thrive where resentment exists. Colossians 3:13 reminds us to *"bear with each other and forgive one another if any of you has a grievance against someone. Forgive as the Lord forgave you."* This verse became a foundation for our marriage, reminding us that if we wanted to move forward in unity, forgiveness and grace had to be practiced daily.

Ultimately, putting closure to the past is about choosing love over frustration, healing over resentment, and resolution over lingering bitterness. When couples make peace with their past, they create space for deeper intimacy, trust, and joy in the future. Every marriage will experience struggles, but by actively choosing to close doors on past conflicts, couples give themselves the opportunity to build a stronger, healthier, and more fulfilling relationship.

Holding onto old wounds, resentments, and unresolved tensions can quietly erode trust and connection, making it difficult for couples to move forward in unity. Closure is not just about forgetting the past—it's about resolving it in a way that strengthens the future. Without actively choosing to address lingering issues, we risked allowing them to create distance between us.

Even when couples move forward, unresolved issues can create silent emotional barriers in a marriage. These unresolved tensions may not be openly discussed, but they often manifest in subtle ways—like defensiveness in conversations, hesitancy in expressing needs, or overreacting to minor issues. Past conflicts sometimes influenced our reactions even when the current discussion isn't directly related to them.

Apologies are valuable, but they are only the first step in fully closing the door on a conflict. Genuine resolution comes not just from verbalizing regret but from actively rebuilding trust and demonstrating change. If forgiveness is given but the actions remain the same, the conflict has not truly been resolved.

One of the most damaging habits in marriage is bringing up past mistakes to justify frustration in a current disagreement. Referencing old conflicts during new discussions only made it harder to resolve the present issue. Instead of saying, *"You've always done this before,"* we had to shift our conversations toward constructive resolution without revisiting past wounds.

Closure doesn't mean forgetting—it means choosing to move forward instead of allowing past challenges to

Putting Closure To The Past

define the present. Some people believe that letting go of past conflicts requires forgetting them altogether, but true closure means acknowledging what happened while choosing not to let it control the future. We've embraced the mindset that past challenges shaped us but do not dictate our ability to grow together.

In some cases, couples struggle to move forward because they don't create an intentional moment of closure. Symbolic gestures—like praying together, writing down frustrations and tearing them up, or verbally affirming our commitment to fresh starts—help solidify a sense of renewal in our relationship. Taking an active approach to marking new beginnings prevents lingering resentment from affecting future interactions.

Fully closing the door on past struggles creates space for deeper trust and connection. Every time you truly let go of an old disagreement, your will feel lighter, more unified, and more confident in your love. When couples clear past frustrations, they make room for more joy, laughter, and ease in their daily interactions.

Ultimately, putting closure to the past is about choosing love over frustration, healing over resentment, and resolution over lingering bitterness. When couples make peace with their past, they create space for deeper intimacy, trust, and joy in the future. Every marriage will experience struggles, but by actively choosing to close doors on past conflicts, couples give themselves the opportunity to build a stronger, healthier, and more fulfilling relationship.

Even when couples move forward, unresolved issues can create silent emotional barriers in a marriage. These unresolved tensions may not be openly discussed, but they often manifest in subtle ways—like defensiveness in conversations, hesitancy in expressing needs, or overreacting to minor issues. Past conflicts sometimes can influence your reactions even when the current discussion isn't directly related to them.

Apologies are valuable, but they are only the first step in fully closing the door on a conflict. Genuine resolution comes not just from verbalizing regret but from actively rebuilding trust and demonstrating change. If forgiveness is given but the actions remain the same, the conflict has not truly been resolved.

One of the most damaging habits in marriage is bringing up past mistakes to justify frustration in a current disagreement. Referencing old conflicts during new discussions only makes it harder to resolve the present issue. Instead of saying, *"You've always done this before,"* we had to shift our conversations toward constructive resolution without revisiting past wounds.

Some people believe that letting go of past conflicts requires forgetting them altogether, but true closure means acknowledging what happened while choosing not to let it define the future. Past challenges shaped us but do not control our ability to grow together.

In some cases, couples struggle to move forward because they don't create an intentional moment of closure. Symbolic gestures—like praying together, writing down frustrations and tearing them up, or verbally affirming our commitment to fresh starts—help solidify a sense of renewal in our relationship.

Fully closing the door on past struggles creates space for deeper trust and connection. Every time you truly let go of an old disagreement, your will feel lighter, more unified, and more confident in your love. When couples clear past frustrations, they make room for more joy, laughter, and ease in their daily interactions.

Here are some practical tips for putting closure to the past and ensuring that unresolved conflicts do not interfere with the health of your marriage:

TIPS TO REMEMBER:

1. Acknowledge What Happened Without Letting It Define the Future

Recognizing past conflicts is important but reliving them repeatedly will only cause emotional distance. Once an issue is resolved, revisiting it only stirred up unnecessary frustration.

- **Tip:** Have one final conversation about the issue, and once you both commit to closure, let it go completely instead of bringing it up in future discussions.

2. Identify If Any Lingering Resentment Remains

Sometimes, conflicts seem resolved on the surface, but hidden resentment lingers.

- **Tip:** Ask yourself, *Do I still feel bitterness about this?* If the answer is yes, it means true closure hasn't happened yet. Address it openly rather than carrying emotional baggage into future conversations.

3. Focus on Solutions Instead of Just Emotions

While it's important to express hurt feelings, resolution happens when couples focus on how to prevent the same issue from happening again.

- **Tip:** Instead of dwelling on what went wrong, focus on creating new habits, systems, or boundaries that prevent future frustrations.

4. Give Each Other the Benefit of the Doubt

Holding onto the past often comes from assuming that mistakes were intentional rather than human errors.

Choosing to believe the best in each other rather than assuming the worst will help to move forward faster.

- **Tip:** Instead of thinking, *They did this to hurt me,* reframe it as *This wasn't their intention, but how can we prevent it next time?*

5. Practice Symbolic Closure

Sometimes, creating a symbolic moment of closure helps couples truly mark the end of an issue and start fresh.

- **Tip:** Consider writing down past frustrations and tearing them up, praying together for renewal, or verbally affirming a new beginning to ensure emotional healing.

6. Replace Negative Memories with New Positive Experiences

If past conflicts caused emotional distance, creating new positive experiences helps rebuild closeness.

- **Tip:** If an argument made certain places or topics feel negative, redefine them with new joyful experiences that replace tension with connection.

7. Commit to Growth, Not Perfection

No marriage is without struggles but choosing to grow rather than hold onto resentment allows couples to build something stronger over time. Closure doesn't mean pretending mistakes never happened—it means learning from them and moving forward with wisdom and grace.

- **Tip:** Make a commitment together to handle future conflicts with patience and understanding, ensuring past frustrations don't control your marriage.

CONCLUSION

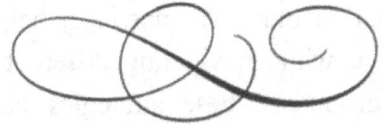

Through the pages of this book, we've explored what it truly means to stand together in love—especially when faced with conflict. We've walked through real-life examples, many of which are familiar struggles for couples everywhere. The disagreements, the frustrations, the moments when emotions run high—all of these are part of every relationship. But the difference between relationships that thrive and those that falter lies in how we handle conflict, not whether it exists.

The stories and strategies shared throughout this book have helped bring clarity to the most common issues couples face. We've learned that disagreements don't have to push partners apart—in fact, when handled with wisdom and care, they can create deeper

Conclusion

understanding, stronger communication, and a greater sense of unity.

One of the greatest takeaways is that love should always rule over conflict. Conflict is a temporary challenge, but love is the foundation that keeps a relationship standing through every storm. It's not about proving who is right—it's about choosing each other over the argument, every single time.

We also introduced three key strategies that have been essential in our own marriage, helping us raise seven children while navigating different cultural and ethnic backgrounds. These strategies have not only brought clarity but have strengthened our ability to communicate, resolve issues, and grow together.

The 30-Minute Thursdays technique has given us space to discuss concerns intentionally rather than impulsively. Setting aside dedicated time for conversations ensures that we talk when emotions are settled rather than reacting in frustration.

The 90/10 Rule reminded us that love must always be bigger than any concern. By ensuring that 90% of our conversations focus on appreciation, warmth, and positivity, with only 10% dedicated to addressing challenges, we condition our minds to view our relationship through a lens of love rather than frustration.

The Planting the Seed method taught us that introducing concerns lightly and allowing time for reflection works far better than demanding immediate explanations. Instead of pushing for answers, we learned to trust that thoughtful communication allows growth to happen naturally.

Through these techniques and lessons, we have discovered that conflict is not the enemy—it is an opportunity for growth. It is a chance to listen more deeply, to understand more fully, and to strengthen the bond between two people who have chosen to build a life together.

At the heart of it all, this book has reaffirmed one simple truth: love, when nurtured with patience and wisdom, will alwys be greater than any disagreement.

Conclusion

REFERENCES

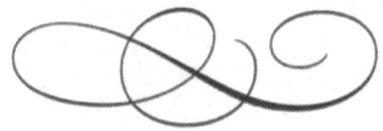

Johnson, K. D., & Green, T. R. (2020). The psychology of interpersonal conflict resolution. *Journal of Relationship Dynamics, 30*(1), 89–102.

Johnson, K. D., & Green, T. R. (2021). The psychology of interpersonal conflict resolution. *Journal of Relationship Dynamics, 29*(2), 114–128.

Markman, H. J., Stanley, S. M., & Blumberg, S. L. (2020). Fighting for your marriage: Proven strategies for effective conflict resolution. Pearson Press.

Smith, R. J., Williams, M. L., & Thompson, A. F. (2022). The impact of effective communication in marital satisfaction. *Journal of Marriage Studies, 35*(4), 213–230.

Smith, R. J., Williams, M. L., & Thompson, A. F. (2022). The impact of effective communication in marital satisfaction. *Journal of Marriage Studies, 36*(2), 198–215.

Williams, B. T., & Thompson, C. R. (2021). Navigating conflict in long-term relationships: Practical strategies for emotional resilience. *Interpersonal Communication Review, 15*(4), 77–91.

www.ingramcontent.com/pod-product-compliance
Lightning Source LLC
Chambersburg PA
CBHW010248010526
44119CB00054B/768